BECOMING YOUR BEST SELF

Healing through self-integration

porter hughes

ISBN 978-0-9958646-2-7

Published by:

porter hughes

porterhughes.com

Illustrations © Isaeva Anna, lolya1988, Artishok, Kovalov Anatolii, Nikolaev Art, advent, ARTBALANCE, iunewind, Eternal Monday / shutterstock.com

Printed in Canada.

First Edition

Visit **donnajacobs.ca**

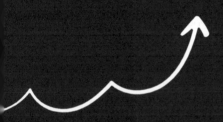

BECOMING YOUR BEST SELF

Healing through self-integration

DONNA JACOBS M.A., C. PSYCH. with SARA GARDNER

ACKNOWLEDGMENTS

To Stevie—Not only have you always been the solid ground beneath my feet, but you have also been the wind beneath my wings. Thank you for the ability to rely on you and for helping me soar and grow. Thank you for reading the manuscript and offering your wisdom. You are my perfect partner and my best friend.

To Jamie and Tracy—You both share a place in my heart as my two darling daughters and my dearest friends. You have always been my fans and supported my endeavours however wacky they were. Thank you for believing in me.

To my family of origin—for providing me with a context to understand my psychology and my adaptations, and to grow from them.

To Suzanne—my fearless project leader. Thank you for coming to my workshop, getting inspired, taking me under your wing and convincing me that we had something here that was valuable to pass on. For all your guidance and support and calming influence. I will always credit you as my launching pad.

To Sara—You have been such an integral part of this process. I gave you my creation and you lovingly and skillfully managed to know exactly how to keep the tenor of my voice. Your magic at reworking text, organizing, formatting, and adding story and context have all elevated the book to new heights. I am so grateful to have such an effortless working relationship with you.

To Deirdre—I knew what my book looked like before the content was written. I envisioned what the book would feel like to hold, I leafed through the pages in my mind. I was able to see font, white space, pictorial icons and layout. And somehow you must have taken a photograph of the pictures in my mind when I wasn't looking, because your design *is* my vision. I thank you for your amazing talent.

To all my first draft readers Kyra, Adam, Linda, Lawrence, Ellen. Thank you all so much for so graciously accepting to read the draft. Your time, observations, and input have helped bring us closer to the final product.

To my peer reviewers—Steve, Janet and Shelley. Thank you all for taking the time to read the manuscript and give your feedback. You were all an integral part of shaping the finished product with your keen, clinical eyes.

To Melanie—my right-hand gal. You have been with me now for almost a decade and I can't imagine life without you. Thank you for your belief in me and for all the help in supporting this project and compiling the list for the email blast.

To John—I can't thank you enough for all of the hours you put in to the grammar, syntax and style edit. You laboured over the text with a keen set of eyes.

To all my brave clients both past and current with whom I have had the pleasure and honour to work. You all have helped demonstrate the power of acknowledging the parts in us that need help. Thank you so much for inspiring me and showing me the way. It is because of all of you that this project has come to fruition. I learn from each and every one of you every day. You have provided the heart and soul of the book.

Donna Jacobs, M.A., C PSYCH.

I would like to thank Donna first and foremost for inspiring me to be my best self—both for those who are in my life but especially for myself. I feel fortunate our paths have crossed, and grateful that you trusted me to help put your ideas to paper. Thank you to Deirdre for elevating our words and ensuring they resonate on the page and linger in our minds. I am forever grateful to Suzanne who encourages us to imagine our brightest dreams and then knows how to help us realize them. Finally, I would like to express gratitude to all my readers who helped me ensure the text did justice to the model, to Joel, Beth, Carrie, Lorraine; and especially to my dad, John Gardner, whose attention to detail and commitment to quality is exacting and—in a different way—has always encouraged me to be my best self.

Sara Gardner

CONTENTS

SECTION I

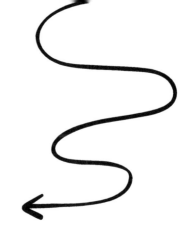

SECTION II

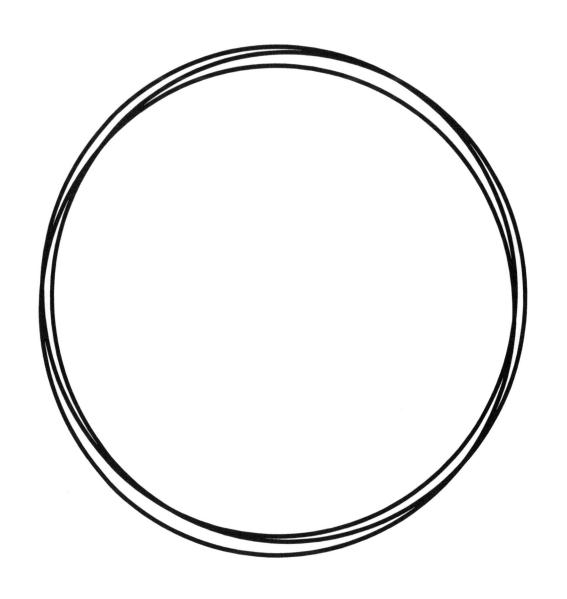

Introduction

Searching for Better
(and where to look)

_____

Over the past forty years, client after client has entered my office, sat across from me, and—in one way or another—asked the same question, "How can my life be better?" Usually they present in a time of crisis. They feel helpless and can't see a way forward. The clouds are heavy, the horizon distant and life is overwhelming.

While I can never alter their life circumstances, I can offer them a gift called agency. When my clients can realize that they already possess the power to alter their life experiences, they have found agency. I help them realize they will effect change in their lives when they understand that they need to shift the questions to, "How can *I* be a better spouse, daughter, son, parent, employee, boss, writer, artist, athlete?" "How can *I* be a better human?" "How can *I* be a better version of myself?"

People come in with confusion, anger, sadness and other emotions they don't know how to negotiate. Despite each of these stories being unique, the journey towards improving their lives involves the same path; one that follows my *Self-Integration Model* (SIM).

From the information my clients share, I have created personalities for this book. All identifying details have been changed to protect privacy, and their stories have been altered and combined to make entirely new narratives that illustrate our common experiences. Let's meet some of these people whose stories will emerge throughout the text as I explain the model.

Emma is a successful, 44-year-old woman in the midst of her career and raising a family. Nobody would suspect she is profoundly sad. She is beginning to see that she has been living her life for others, compromising her innermost core. She is living a life that checks all the boxes but offers little fulfilment.

Daniel is 37 and wants to understand why he is furious at his father all the time. He says things like, "I can't believe the anger I feel inside." He is angry at home and at his children. The slightest incident at work triggers overreactions, which he knows could cost him his job. He knows this has to stop.

Julia, age 25, feels as if she has no control over her life at all. She feels things never go her way, and that somehow her mom is to blame. In fact, she can't even remember a time when she had a good relationship with either of her moms.

Evan is 32 years old and can't seem to keep a relationship. His partners complain that he's aggressive, even abusive. He doesn't feel as though he's doing anything wrong, but he can't seem to make anything work. He wants help, but at the same time he doesn't actually believe anyone can help him.

Angie, 21, feels that her life is always being derailed. She is certain that if anything bad is going to happen, it will happen to her. She has closed herself off from the possibility of positivity.

These individuals always present with pain, with challenges seemingly so insurmountable they feel they cannot move forward on their own, and desperately want to change the direction their lives are taking. They have come to my office looking for a solution, for something that will improve their lives. As we work together, I am able to show them that what they are looking for, they already possess. They will uncover their own best selves as they practise integrating their lived experiences with their learned behaviours. As they apply this Model to their lives, they will begin to present a better version of themselves to the world.

The *Self-Integration Model* (SIM) grew from my professional training, my years of experience as a therapist and my own introspection. This book describes how I developed the model and explains how it works. It shows how we can apply SIM to give us control over our lives and relationships. I use case studies inspired from my practice and more generalized scenarios to illustrate how we can manage the way we respond to the challenges that life inevitably presents.

The first part of the book explains the model: the parts that make up the Self, its interrelated elements and the context in which these function. This section explores SIM's fundamental concepts, including the family of origin, our *adaptations* and the different parts of our personality. Our personalities will be examined through our internal Parent, Adult and Child States where these are understood to be distinct from the external parent, adults and children in our lives. These States refer instead to internal filter and response systems through which we experience the world. The second part of the book explains the 6 step healing process, using examples of real people as they work through the model and effect change in their lives. The appendix offers a series of worksheets that can support us as we work through the steps. By applying the model to our own lives, we can work at becoming our best selves.

Leaving Montreal
(at the end, a beginning)

I sealed the box with packing tape, protecting the dollhouse the girls and I had spent the better part of the year refinishing, and looked around the empty house. We were finally ready for the move. My husband had left a year earlier, shortly after Quebec's second failed independence referendum. 1995 saw the greatest voter turnout in provincial electoral history with the "no" side eking out a victory by the narrowest of margins. Although Quebec would remain within Canada's fold, the rising popularity of the separatist movement fed an atmosphere of uncertainty that drove many anglophones to seek a more secure future elsewhere in the country. My family would do the same.

We were one of the last from our group of friends to relocate. Many from our circle had left Montreal after the first referendum in 1980. Having been born and raised in Montreal I was loath to leave. Montreal was my home, and I had imagined I would live my whole life there. I had my family, my friends, a full life and a thriving private psychology practice. Our daughters loved Montreal and were also building their lives there.

My husband, Steve, had always been eager to make the move; he was ready to lay the groundwork for us in Toronto, Ontario. He left in the fall soon after the referendum, but we decided that the girls and I would stay back, allowing them to finish out their school year and give me the time necessary to wind up my practice.

The day Steve pulled out of the driveway to head west on highway 401, the girls and I turned to each other and quickly understood we had an adventure before us. Eager to fill the void left by his departure, we immediately got to work. We pulled out a tired dollhouse from our daughters' early childhood and set to the task of rebuilding it. Our need to nest saw us finding new furniture, replacing the existing wallpaper, gluing pieces that were coming unhinged. We repaired and redecorated that dollhouse until it looked better than it had when we had first purchased it. Even at the time, the metaphor of our work was not lost on us. We were nurturing a growing sense of opportunity. Our excitement about a new home and a new life in Toronto was growing. What I did not yet know was how this move would afford me the opportunity to define a model that would drive my overarching approach to therapy.

The year passed quickly with Steve returning home almost every weekend to spend time with us. I found that I had mixed feelings about the move. I was sad and emotional about what we were losing—I was about to leave all that I had built, leaving me feeling insecure and regretful. I was nervous and afraid, and could hear myself fearing the worst: "What if no one calls me?" "What if I can't build a practice in Toronto?" "OMG, I'm leaving everything I have built behind. What's going to happen?" You will see later in this book how recognizing these feelings and monologues became an important part of building my therapeutic model.

On the one hand, it was especially difficult to tell my parents and my clients of my approaching departure. On the other hand, I was excited about the new adventure, and the closer we got to the moving date, the more excited the girls and I were becoming. Our finale came on a Friday with the girls attending their last day of school and me on stage with my band singing a final gig on the Saturday night. The moving van was loaded bright and early the next morning, and we waved goodbye to our home. We were off!

The Beginning of My Practice
(transactional analysis—an overview)

Healing starts with a wound. Early on in my practice, I came to realize that each one of my clients presented with a wound. These wounds are our problematic feelings, which reside in what I refer to as the Child State, the place where we feel.

All kinds of hurt walked through my door. Addicted, depressed, anxious, lacking in confidence, unemployed, suffering a loss, in conflict with others, traumatized, having affairs, dying, feeling inadequate, hopeless, helpless, entitled, jealous, selfish, guilty, victimized, fearful, immobilized or shamed. No one comes for therapy because they feel confident, happy, hopeful or empowered. Instead they come with a wound, which is fuelled by what I refer to as a Parent or Filter State. It could be the actual parent who raised us, or—once we leave our family of origin—the way we have assumed the role of parent and have parented ourselves. As my professional experience grew, so did the profound realization that in order for any of us to be the best version of ourselves, we needed to heal the Inner Child first, and learn to parent ourselves in a healthy way.

Eric Berne developed the concepts underpinning the therapeutic model known as Transactional Analysis (TA). He proposed that there are three ego states that govern the way we present ourselves to the world—the parent, the adult and the child (PAC). The Parent, Adult, Child States are easily identified, particularly represented by the three circles of self shown here.

Becoming our best selves means listening to the child within.

The Self-Integration Model (SIM) offers two important insights into a therapeutic approach that applies these ego states. First, it elaborates on Berne's earlier use of the Parent, Adult and Child states. Second, it directs our attention inwardly to heal ourselves before we consider our external relationships.

Berne proposes that our Parent State *teaches*, our Adult State *learns* and our Child State *feels*. SIM puts forward the variety of ways that these states carry out their functions, clarifying the complicated internal dynamic that takes place as we process experience. I reframe Berne's proposition as well as those of the more modern Transactional Analysis followers, and suggest that the Parent State filters, the Adult State takes care of business, and the Child State feels. In accordance with many psychological theories, the Child State, which develops at a very young age, harbours our raw emotions and holds our wounds. Regardless of our age, we never lose this Child State that forms an essential part of us. We have to assume that, even as we reach our 60s, 70s, 80s and 90s, we will continue to feel emotions such as joy, happiness, anxiety, enthusiasm, self-doubt, selfishness, spontaneity, confidence and a whole array of other feelings that make up our lived experience. In my practice, over and over again, I would see that it was my clients' Child State that needed attention.

As a therapist, I was attracted to an approach that diverged from traditional methods, which assumed much of our psyche is unconscious and thus out of reach. Early psychotherapy leaned on Freud's model of personality, purporting that our Id, our most instinctual drive, is unconscious and could only be accessed through years of psychoanalysis, dream interpretation, free association and hypnosis. Although my orientation includes a strong psychodynamic element, which believes in unconscious and subconscious motivations that are open to our consciousness, Berne's approach was appealing because it identified specific parts of the self and opened up access to these conscious parts that would lead to effective outcomes in therapy. I wanted to empower my clients with tools to access their feelings, their behaviours, their personalities.

Since Berne's Transactional Analysis, there have been many other models of therapy that have influenced my thinking. Relationship models, such as Terry Real's Relational Life Therapy, have been important as they address the concept of Inner Child and focus on presenting our best versions of self in our relationships. The Inner Child models acknowledge the importance of recognizing and healing the Child within. Attachment Theory models take into account the importance of early relationships and the impact of these primary attachments on our future relationships. I consider SIM to be a relationship model as well. By re-parenting our Inner Child, we teach ourselves how to be in relationship with all of our healthy parts in order to be better partners, parents and friends. Once we recognize the unconscious and subconscious factors that motivate us, SIM contends that if all parts of the self are open to our consciousness, we are then equipped with the ability to change the way we feel. We can be the agents of our own change and SIM can pave our way forward.

What does it mean to self-integrate? Self-integration relies on the notion that when we recognize unhealthy parts of the Self and learn how they contribute to our unhappiness, we can begin to override these negative influences. We can begin to self-integrate by incorporating the healthier parts—those we already possess—into our understanding of the Self and into our interactions within our environments. To integrate is to take the best parts of ourselves and become solid and authentic in our core, independent of outside forces. Only when we learn how to become the best version of ourselves within, can we offer our better selves to external relationships.

Transactional Analysis planted the seedlings for my model; it identified the tangible parts of our personality that are readily accessible. Years of clinical practice offered me the opportunity to witness the various Parent, Adult and Child States of clients that entered my office. It allowed me to develop a deeper understanding of my own personal story and also, to see new areas of opportunity in Berne's model. My primary focus became how we parent our own Inner Child in order to be healthy, to feel fulfilled, to be positive, to be constructive in our own lives, and to self-integrate. Over the years, my clients continually demonstrated to me that the work we were doing on the inside was where the war was to be won. Understanding how we parent ourselves, once we leave our family of origin, is crucial to healing and becoming our best selves.

Family of Origin
(understanding its formative power and our own agency)

Family of Origin refers to the family dynamic within which we were raised. Who were the people in the family? Who were the key people responsible for raising me? What were the relationships between the family members?

To say that we are each impacted—in one way or another—by our past is certain. To say however that we are all solely products of our past would be limiting, robbing us of the power of agency in our own lives. Our childhoods—the interactions we have had with members of our families and our shared, lived experiences—form the stage on which each of us learns about ourselves and about our relationships with others. Our families of origin script a template for the way we position ourselves in the world, both positively and negatively. While we can accept the reality of this truth, I propose that as each of us leaves our family of origin, we also have the power to shift our position, change the script, and redefine our roles and stances.

As a little girl growing up, whether I realized it at the time or not, I was absorbing my family dynamics. My family had many strengths. The weak point was the tension felt between my mother and my brother. I could hear my parents fighting about what was the best parental strategy for him. I watched as my father set no boundaries for him, and observed the dynamic between my mother and brother escalate. My father had the last word and believed by providing everything and anything for my brother, he would help him overcome his failing grades and behavioural issues. What no one knew at the time was that my brother struggled with undiagnosed learning disabilities and undiagnosed ADHD.

I witnessed my mother's helplessness and fear grow, and I began shaping how I would fit into this web of relationships. As a result of what I saw in the relationships around me, I adopted the role of the "good girl." I did not want to add any more distress to the family so I became the "golden child." I did well in school, I had lots of friends and I learned not to disappoint anyone, especially not my parents. I didn't know how to say "no," so I pleased. I asked for nothing. And, I became afraid. Afraid to displease, afraid to say no, afraid of people not liking me. I would be the good girl. I would wear my halo. And my halo would shine brightly.

It is important to state that depending on the personality of the child, a parent might exercise a very different Parent State for each of their own children. Self-Integration Model (SIM) identifies six Parent States or filters which will be elaborated on in the first section of this book. In describing my family of origin I will reference some of the parent concepts that played a role in my upbringing.

As I demanded very little from my parents, my father was the epitome of the Protective and Nurturing Parent to me, differing his approach dramatically from the role of the overly Indulgent Parent he played for my brother. Meanwhile my mother could be a fun-loving Child for me since I demanded little and she saw me as no threat. My mother, who was used to receiving enormous amounts of attention from my father, was beginning to view my brother as competition. To my brother, she became the Critical Parent. The stage was set. Here was the standoff.

As a child of the '60s, I would eventually exchange my good girl persona for one of rebellion. What I didn't realize at the time was that

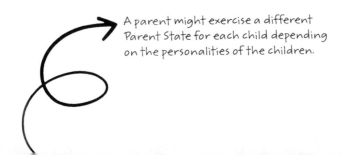

A parent might exercise a different Parent State for each child depending on the personalities of the children.

this newly formed "lost girl" was desperately trying to find her "self," a "self," any "self." Somewhere deep down inside she may have realized that both roles compromised her inner core; she was neither the perfect child nor the daring rebel. I was not self-integrated. I remained distant from my own Child State. Only when I took myself to therapy at the age of twenty-one did I begin to realize the impact of my family and the roles I had assumed, neither of which resonated with my authentic Self. I was curious, and always had been and I slowly began to put the pieces together.

Many influences cross our paths through life, but the most significant ones are those people who raise us in our formative years. SIM grew from an understanding that who we are has everything to do with from whence we came. Our feelings—including those of anger, hopelessness, frustration, anxiety—our reactions, our ways of dealing with conflict, our ability to read others and respond accordingly—all of these were learned during the initial stages where our stories began.

The ways that we learned to behave are called our adaptations. We behave and react as we did in our families of origin without realizing that the cast of characters has changed and that we no longer need to use these adaptations in the same way. Adaptations are essential tools for survival as we learn to adapt to our families of origin. As we mature, however, we leave the nest, we strike out on our own and we form new relationships—at work, with friends, in new family units. Despite our new environments, many of us continue to carry with us our old toolkit of adaptations, ones that perhaps bear little relevance to our new lives. Yet, I contend, if we apply our understanding of self-integration, we become empowered. We recognize that we have the ability to control how we filter experiences, to modify our adaptations, to change the way we negotiate relationships, and to reposition ourselves as we face the world.

My departure from Transactional Analysis begins here. Berne's model presents as a relationship theory, analysing transactions between people. I, on the other hand, ask us to examine our *internal* transactions. First, we need to understand how we are parenting ourselves, parenting our own Inner Child. If we can understand our families of origin and how we are affected by those years of experience, we can begin to understand how to re-parent ourselves, heal our wounds and equip ourselves with new adaptations. We can choose how to interact with the world. It was lightning in a bottle and I knew it because it was happening to me.

As my understanding of psychology grew, I began to acknowledge the Child I carried within me. I learned to recognize her adaptations, those she had developed from her family of origin. I saw how anxious she was feeling—worried that someone would be angry with her, scared to try new things, afraid to rock the boat. I saw that I had been so intent on pleasing others that I hadn't even noticed that the Child inside of me was lost. Fear can take on many shapes—both internal and external. By virtue of being raised in a family where "everything was dangerous," my fear transferred to external events as well. I was afraid to try new things, afraid to push the envelope, afraid to step out of my comfort zone.

Equipped with my training and professional experience and with my own personal therapy, I was determined to search inwards. I began to realize that my Inner Child had no reason to be afraid and could ask for what she wanted and needed. Her adaptations were old and no longer relevant to her maturing self, the one living outside the family where she had grown up. When I examined my place in the world, I could see that I had emerged into adulthood strong, independent and motivated. I decided that I needed to address the needs of the Inner Child I was just starting to see. I asked myself what I could do to challenge my Inner Child and allow her to prove to herself that she was strong. I realized that I had two monologues playing in my head. One was driven by a lineage of previous generations in my family convincing me that "everything was dangerous," which caused insecurity and

Once we leave our family of origin it is no longer about blame, but about curiosity, insight and change.

self-doubt. I became risk-averse. The other was making me nervous by catastrophizing that bad things would happen. These two versions of anxiety seemed to cover all the bases. I was afraid to try new things, and I was afraid to find my voice and stand up for my little girl.

To address the first version of anxiety that feared perceived risk, I worked at re-parenting myself through the self-integration process. On my fiftieth birthday, to celebrate this work, I presented my little girl, my Inner Child, with a gift. I said to her, "You are no longer going to be afraid." The next month I went out and got my motorcycle licence!

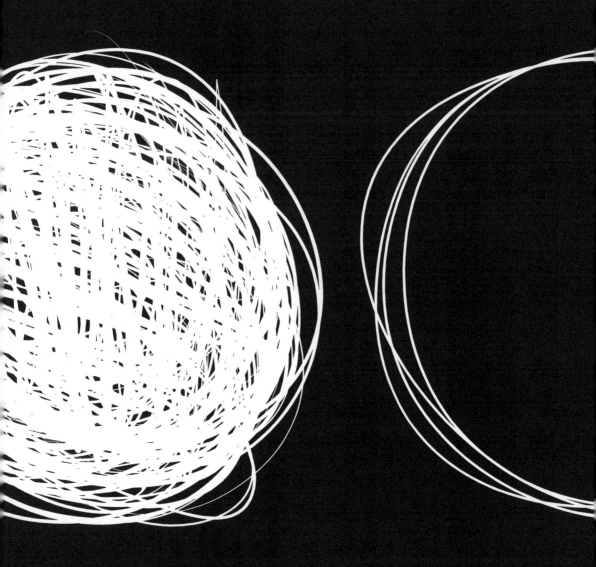

SECTION 1

SELF-INTEGRATION MODEL

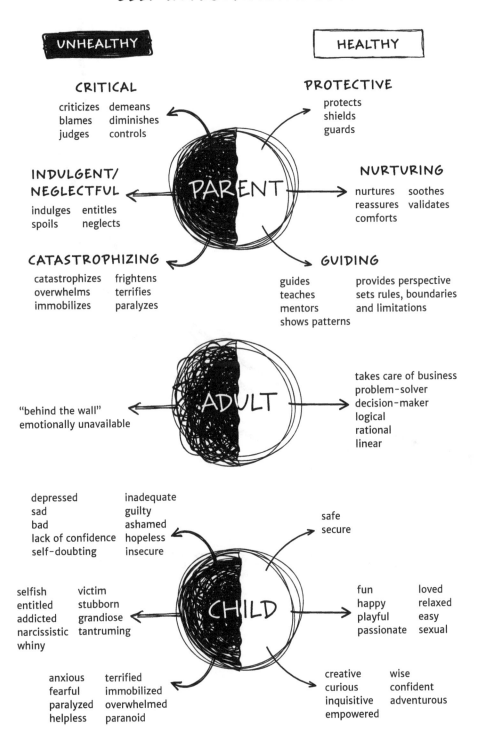

CRITICAL

criticizes   demeans
blames   diminishes
judges   controls

PROTECTIVE

protects
shields
guards

INDULGENT/ NEGLECTFUL

indulges   entitles
spoils   neglects

NURTURING

nurtures   soothes
reassures   validates
comforts

CATASTROPHIZING

catastrophizes   frightens
overwhelms   terrifies
immobilizes   paralyzes

GUIDING

guides   provides perspective
teaches   sets rules, boundaries
mentors   and limitations
shows patterns

PARENT

ADULT

"behind the wall"
emotionally unavailable

takes care of business
problem-solver
decision-maker
logical
rational
linear

depressed   inadequate
sad   guilty
bad   ashamed
lack of confidence hopeless
self-doubting   insecure

safe
secure

selfish   victim
entitled   stubborn
addicted   grandiose
narcissistic tantruming
whiny

CHILD

fun   loved
happy   relaxed
playful   easy
passionate sexual

anxious   terrified
fearful   immobilized
paralyzed   overwhelmed
helpless   paranoid

creative   wise
curious   confident
inquisitive adventurous
empowered

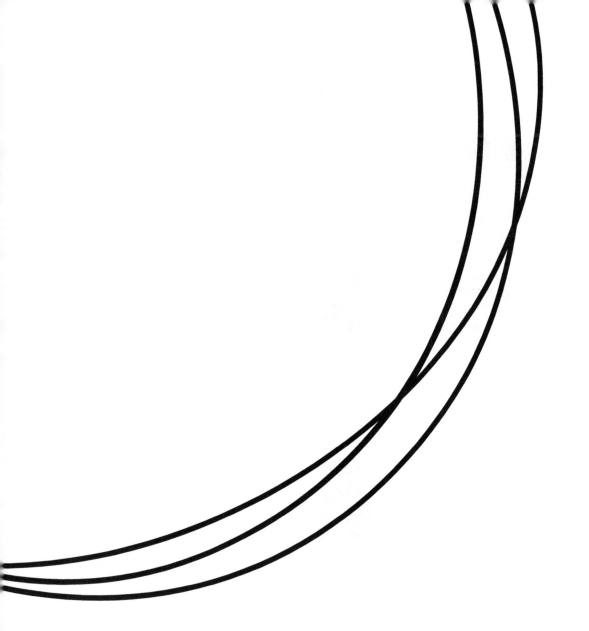

The Self-Integration Model

Its framework

Parents and Filters
(recognizing who's on board)

When we made the move to Toronto, I reached out to my network to prepare as soft a landing as possible. A close friend of mine from childhood had set up a therapy practice in Toronto. It had been a few years since we had spoken but she opened her arms to me, offering me space in her own co-practice with other psychologists and psychotherapists. This new community helped orient me to the psychology scene in my new city.

I was now part of a practising group of therapists. I not only brought my expertise to them, but also drank in their focus as I learned about their therapeutic approaches. With the concept of the Inner Child firmly in place, I further developed the Self-Integration Model. I elaborated on the concepts of the Inner Child, family of origin and healing. My emerging clinical model was also influenced by Leonard Shaw's work on love and forgiveness. Another great influence was Terry Real whose model of Relational Life Therapy (RLT) and his work in healing the Inner Child continue to inspire me today. Through these influences, I knew I was on the right track in developing a model that intuitively spoke to me. It became clear to me that in order to be the best versions of ourselves, we would need to start by healing the Inner Child.

The Child State is the place in our personality where we feel. Every feeling resides in our Child State. It is the warehouse of all of our needs and wants. In addition, the Child in each of us reacts to the psychological state of the Parent it faces. Each of these Parent States evokes distinct feelings in the Child. It is our Parent State that filters how we perceive things and ultimately how we feel about them. As a child, if we were to fall, a Critical Parent might scold us and make us feel silly or inadequate for being clumsy. After a failure, a Nurturing Parent could make us feel proud or brave for having tried. I consider these Parent States the filters by which we perceive our real-life experiences.

In my practice, I help clients acknowledge their own Inner Child, understand their families of origin and label their accompanying adaptations. We work together to begin the healing process, and to learn to choose which Parent to bring on board in order to re-parent the Inner Child and ultimately to heal. I see that the wounds my clients present to me in their Child States form very defined groups of feelings, each group directly related to a particular Parent State.

SIM identifies six Parent States, three residing in what I refer to as the Unhealthy side—the Critical, the Indulgent/Neglectful and the Catastrophizing Parents—and three in what I refer to as the Healthy side—the Protective, the Nurturing and the Guide. The ultimate goal of the model is to learn how to parent oneself from the healthy side of the model since each Parent—or filter—corresponds to an equivalent Child State and related set of feelings. I like to call it the *handshake*.

Throughout my earlier life, I had allowed my Catastrophizing Parent to torment my Inner Child, rendering her highly anxious. This *handshake* between my Unhealthy Parent and little girl had continued to plague me, convincing me that if I found my voice, said what I thought, or displeased someone, the results would be catastrophic. To heal this second version of my anxiety, I was able, with a lot of hard work, to bring my Healthy Parents on board and break the Unhealthy handshake that was causing me that unnecessary anxiety.

SCENARIO:
An example of how two of the six different parent filters can perceive a flat tire

You are driving out to meet friends at a music festival. You've hopped on the highway and are making good time, which is great because you got a late start. Suddenly, your car starts to drag to one side and is hard to handle. You've got a flat! You're able to pull over safely and get out to inspect the car. Let's look at how two different types of Parent States filter the situation and affect how we might deal with it.

The CATASTROPHIZING PARENT
When faced with a flat tire, we can panic and allow our Catastrophizing Parent to hook its grips into us.

"OMG, I have a flat. What am I going to do? I don't know how to change a flat tire and what if it gets dark and no one finds me on this road? Uh-oh, a car has just stopped. Maybe they are dangerous? They're approaching. OMG, what am I going to do? This is terrible!!!!"

The GUIDE
When faced with a flat tire, we can gain perspective from our Guide.

"What a bummer! I have a flat and don't really know how to change a tire. While I can see that it's still light out and the road is well travelled, I also know my initial reaction may be to freak out. As soon as I identify this initial reaction as the Catastrophizing Parent, I can calm down and think clearly. I'm a member of CAA. I can call them, and lock the car doors until they arrive. Even if I have to wait two hours, it's a nice day and my phone is well charged, so I have a lot with which to entertain myself."

We see in this example that although the external situation is the same, how we filter it through our Parent States determines the intensity and direction of our response. If we allow the Catastrophizing Parent on board, we are going to feel terrified, helpless, and paralyzed. If we filter the experience through the Guide, we become empowered, able and confident.

Understanding Parent Filters

The Self-Integration Model features six Parent States through which experiences are filtered. Regardless of how we were parented by our actual parents, we all possess within us each of the six Parent States, whether we are aware of them or not. Some form a prominent part of our personality; some may remain dormant or less evident. Dominant states can present in the Parent filters or elsewhere in a person's personality. For example, a person may have a Critical Parent who is dominant. This person readily filters life's experiences through a critical, negative, judgmental lens. Another might find themselves with a predominant Adult State, focused on taking care of business, or in a predominantly Child State, looking to have fun. Read more about these States in their respective chapters.

In therapy we want to identify the Unhealthy Parents because they are the source of our distress. Depending upon which Parent is on board, we can feel any number of responses: for example, soothed or insecure, guided or lost, motivated or defeated.

In understanding the impact of parenting, we begin with:
→ a consideration of the parents who raised us,
→ an assessment of how we parent our own Inner Child, and finally
→ an examination of how we interact with those around us, and how we parent our own children if we have them

These Parent States are present in each of us and are evident in our relationships with others and also in our relationship with ourselves. Even very young children, by age six, begin exercising their Parent States.

Traditionally we develop our Parent States from exposure to the parents in our own lives. We either model the parenting we experienced as children, or we react against it. For example, we see our father rage anytime someone questions his authority, and now we do the same because we never learned appropriate ways of dealing with frustration or with feeling out of control. Alternatively, we could see this same parent raging, and we withdraw, shutting down and vowing never to rage against anyone. In this latter case, we may never learn appropriate expressions of feelings or to find our voice. Recognizing how we are filtering experiences—seeing which parent is on board—allows us to understand the emotional response felt by the Inner Child.

GENERATIONS OF P A C

Each individual has their own PAC represented below by equal states. In reality, a person's PAC is represented with circles of varying sizes. One's predominant state is captured by a larger symbol while the more dormant state is shown with a smaller circle. Regardless of the dominant state, the P is always on top, the Adult in the middle, and the Child on the bottom.

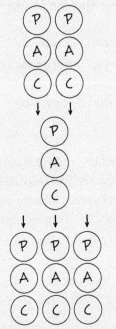

Our parents/guardians who raised us (each has their own P A C)

We understand our parent's predominant state and how we were affected, and we look at whether we reacted against it or borrowed their style. Here, for simplicity's sake, Parents are represented as two individuals when in reality many of us are raised in single family homes or by a multitude of guardians.

Ourselves (re-parenting ourselves)

We look at our own personal make up. What state is our predominant state? How do we parent ourselves?

How we parent our children (and interact with others)

How do we interact with others? If we have children, how do we parent them? Is it similar to how we were parented? Is it different from how we parent ourselves? What do we have to change?

See p. 60 for an example. Go to worksheet on p. 123 to trace your generations of P A C.

Triggers: External Situations or Internal Filters?

Life can be hard. Life can throw difficult situations our way that challenge us each day. These external events or triggers can cause us to feel a whole host of emotions, including pain, discomfort, anger, resentment, fear or insecurity. Before we even get to work in the morning, we might have already experienced any number of upsetting circumstances. For example:

→ Your kids won't get ready for school, leading you to feel stressed and frustrated.

→ Your partner was distracted by the phone, while you scrambled to get everyone out the door, leaving you feeling ticked off.

→ Your mother called asking when she was going to see you since it's already been too many lonely days, filling you with guilt.

→ Your rideshare called to say he's sick and that he won't be driving today, leaving you panicked.

And it's only 7:58!

Inevitably these types of external situations occur, and we have to acknowledge that they will have an impact on how we feel. Although the external situations are real, it is our very own Parent or Filter System which is informing our reaction and its intensity. To determine whether we should be concerned by the intensity and nature of our

When we learn to recognize which parent is on board, we are better able to unpack and manage how we are feeling.

reaction to an external event, we can measure the intensity of the external event's impact over us. We can ask ourselves what power the event on its own *should* have over us, and contrast it with the actual intensity we are feeling. If there is a great disparity, we need to pause and examine our filter system. We can rank the intensity of our reactions out of 10 to help us assess our reactions. For example, being late on its own might cause us to react at a 2 out of 10, but when filtered through a Catastrophizing Parent who panics that our job is at stake, we might feel the intensity of our reaction at an 8 or 9. This is when we know we need to pause and practise SIM.

SCENARIO:
Filter systems in action

You meet someone on a dating app. You expect them to call. They said they would call. You wait and wait, but don't hear from them. An upsetting situation, maybe a 3 or 4 on the intensity scale. You can choose, however, to filter this situation in ways that can either augment and intensify difficult feelings, or soothe and diminish an existing emotion. Let's try on each of the six filters. In each case, consider how the Inner Child is feeling in response to the Parent filter:

 66 *Of course she didn't call. Why would she call you? What's so special about you? She's probably talking to five other guys who outshine you.*

 66 *Call her. Call her now. It doesn't matter that you've already left 14 messages. Call her!!!*

 66 *What if she calls while you're in the movie? Uh oh, it's a missed call; what if that was her? Maybe you won't hear back from her again. What are you going to do?*

66 Hey, back off _____ (insert any of the Unhealthy Parents.) Enough! Leave him alone. We are done listening to you torment him! Back off! You have no more access to him, from now on you have to come through me! (Notice how this Parent State is protecting the individual from his own negative filter system)

66 It's OK. I know you are really disappointed and wanted her to call. I know you felt you could really have something special with her. You are a warm, loving, lovable guy. I've got you now, whatever happens, it's going to be ok.

66 Let's get some perspective here. You've gone out with her five times. In total you have spent 30 hours with her. Think about what you are attaching to in that time. Relationships need time. You had a life before her and if you never see her again, you will have a life after her. Also, it's an important life skill to be able to hold on to your core self and not compromise it for anyone. We also know that this quick tendency to attach is based on your need to fill your early abandonment wound. Let's work on that.

Next time something bad happens, ask yourself…
"How do I want to do this?"

SCENARIO:
Filter systems in action with a focus on the CRITICAL PARENT

Your husband has had an affair. You, in your rage, have told everyone what he has done. You have been separated for six months. By sharing the many gory details with everyone you know, you have ensured that people are on your side and the world sees him as an evil, narcissistic man. Now you both have decided to try to make it work. However, by villainizing him you have already created much damage to your relationship and his reputation. You want to give it a try, but you feel guilt and shame. Guilt for trashing him so badly. Shame for feeling weak. You fear people will judge you for trying to make it work.

You are undeniably in a difficult situation. Your external situation is tricky as you attempt to chart a new path forward with your partner. But, when your Critical Parent steps up to bat, this external situation becomes unbearable, evoking the shame and guilt that the external reality itself could not do alone. Your Critical Parent tells you things like:

66 *You weakling. Going back after he betrayed you for so long! Where is your pride?*

Have you no self-respect!

What is wrong with you?

Are you that desperate?

What are people going to say?

Your decision to make it work with your husband does not in itself cause shame or guilt. Your Critical Parent, coming on board, filters the situation and is responsible for evoking these negative feelings.

Each day we encounter emotional triggers, which we filter through our Parent States to the Inner Child. These external situations are real and impact us. It is the Parent we choose to bring on board, however, that dictates how we will process the situation and determines how the Child will feel. If we can identify Unhealthy Parent filters and replace them with Healthy Parent alternatives, we can manage how we respond to challenging circumstances.

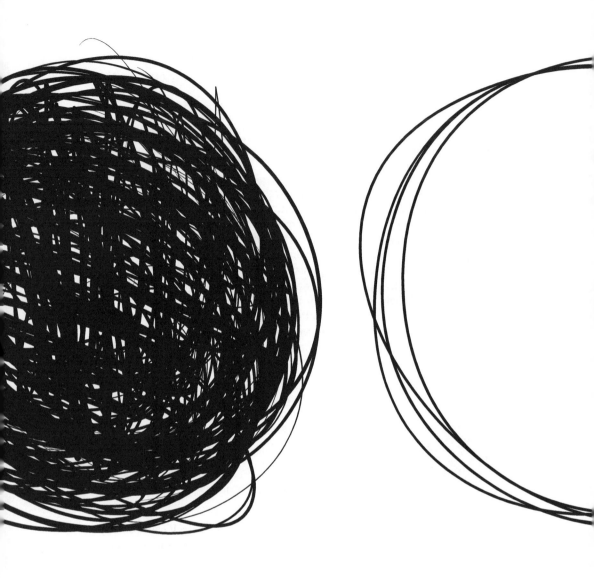

The Model
Feelings, filters and adaptations

The Parent State (filters)

In this section I will outline the six Parent States. Let us begin with our three Unhealthy Parent States.

CRITICAL PARENT

The Critical Parent can be critical to our own self and also to others. This filter is not a healthy state for ourselves nor for our relationships. The Critical Parent has a job to do and its primary purpose is to control.

Anytime you hear yourself or anyone else say the following things, it is the Critical Parent:

 What the hell is the matter with you?

Did you not hear what I said?

We went through this yesterday.

This is full of mistakes!

I don't care about your opinion.

You got an A-? Where's the A+?

What a jerk.

Did you see that guy? What was he thinking?

No wonder you lost your job; you're a bully!

You didn't get the job? Of course you didn't. You're not smart enough. You think you're smart but in reality, people are finding out the truth.

Of course she had an affair. Look at you! You're out of shape. You can't find a job. What do you really have to offer her?

This Parent is harsh. It makes us feel badly about ourselves and badly about the world around us. This Parent's lens is to find fault. It can ruin a beautiful day or a wonderful interaction by looking at the one aspect that was negative. When we have done a good job and might have been proud of our work, this Parent filter will find the one thing we might have done better or differently. It will be sure to tell us all about it. Perhaps we find ourselves having a great time at a party where we connected with all of our friends. We feel great about ourselves, about how we look and carry ourselves, about our social skills and our place in the friend group—until we notice the one person who seemed to avoid us. We filter this one non-interaction as a negative interaction. We have failed to connect with that person; they didn't want to talk to us. Somehow the Critical Parent has filtered this missed connection and allowed it to cloud the whole evening. As an external event, it does not in itself yield much power to make us feel bad.

PARENT functions
The Critical Parent engages in a variety of functions, all of which impact the Inner Child. The Critical Parent:
→ criticizes
→ blames
→ judges
→ demeans
→ diminishes
all with the intent to gain control.

CHILD feelings
Each Parent State function evokes a corresponding feeling in the Child. When the Critical Parent is on board, we feel:

→ bad
→ sad
→ guilty
→ ashamed
→ self-doubt

→ depressed
→ inadequate
→ angry
→ hopeless
→ insecure

Our Child will always respond emotionally to the Parent filter.

CRITICAL PARENT

(P)
(A)
(C)

CASE STUDY:
Identifying and shedding
the CRITICAL PARENT

Let's meet **Emma**, a 44-year-old high-powered lawyer, married to an equal-ly high-powered man. Together, they present as a power couple. They travel, send their two children to private school, attend charity functions and host elaborate dinner parties. Their lives have been ambitiously charted and they are both right on course. But Emma's shiny veneer is beginning to chip away, revealing a long-avoided inner hurt.

Emma comes to therapy with deep sadness, dissatisfaction and unhappiness about where her life is heading. Through therapy she will learn that she is not honouring her core self, her needs, wants and feelings, but is spending her life trying to please her critical father. She struggles with the shame that she feels as she tries to become the woman she thinks her father needs her to be. Emma learned early to compromise her core to satisfy her father, her external Critical Parent, and has continued living a life that is not true to herself.

Emma has always overachieved for the sole purpose of pleasing her father, and yet has never felt she could meet his expectations. She feels that she is never good enough. She doesn't believe in herself. To hide her perceived inad-equacies, Emma has made a pact to never, ever show herself to the world. To cope with a life with a critical father, Emma has developed an adaptation—she has become hard and locked behind a wall.

With time and softening, and by applying the Self-Integration Model to her own lived experience, Emma begins to build an understanding of how toxic her father has been for her. She learns that she has to heal her wound from her father in order to carve out a strong place for herself and be the woman she is truly meant to be. She needs to accept her flaws and limitations without shame. She knows that she needs to help her little girl understand that her father does not get to define her. Instead of dismissing her Inner Child and parenting her-self through her own Critical Parent as her father has done, Emma must open herself to her internal loving parents—her Protective, Nurturing and Guiding Parents. She needs to hear from her little girl in order to know how to re-par-ent herself.

In identifying the Unhealthy Parent on board, Emma has begun her healing process. As she learns to practise SIM, Emma will begin to see who she wants to be for herself.

INDULGENT/NEGLECTFUL PARENT

The Indulgent/Neglectful Parent State is the one that gives in to or neglects the child. This Parent yields to behaviours, stances and beliefs, which sometimes might make us feel good although they are not working to improve our lives and become our best selves. These behaviours show little regard for anything else. The stances enabled by the Indulgent/Neglectful Parent are patterns or attitudes towards how we live our lives, including victim stance, self pitying stance or a stance of grandiosity. By giving in to every request, the Indulgent Parent teaches the Child that it deserves anything it wants, that it can have whatever it desires, even when it is not in its best interest. We can treat our children, address our peers, or parent ourselves in this way. This indulgence is the equivalent of neglect as the Child is not provided with rules, boundaries or limitations, which would offer guidance and security.

Anytime you hear yourself or anyone else say the following things, it is the Indulgent/Neglectful Parent:

66 *I just gave you money last week, but if you need a little more... here you go.*

You want those donuts. Go ahead, eat the dozen.

Go on, tantrum, eventually you'll get what you want.

I'm counting to three. One, two, three. Did you hear me? I said I'm counting to three. One, two, three. I'm going to say it for the last time. I'm counting to three....

I want another drink, even though I've had five! It feels good! Go ahead. Have another drink.

I don't care when you come home.

I'm attracted to him and want to have an affair because it feels good for me. My need to feel good is more important than my partner's feelings.

You aren't happy at this school either? Let me enrol you in another one.

This Parent affords the Child too much power, giving in to destructive behaviours and life stances that do not offer an individual healthy guidance or perspective. By giving in, this Parent is actually neglecting its job as a parent. Drug addictions, alcohol dependencies, sex addictions, affairs, tantrums, pity parties—these all fall under this Parent's jurisdiction. We allow ourselves to engage in behaviours because they feel good without consideration for anything or anybody else. This Parent indulges our privilege to get and have whatever we want. For this reason the Indulgent/Neglectful Parent is the hardest to extinguish. Why? Because the Child feels good and is getting what it wants.

PARENT functions

The Indulgent/Neglectful Parent engages in a variety of functions, all of which impact the Inner Child. The Indulgent/Neglectful Parent:

→ spoils → neglects
→ gives in → victimizes
→ indulges → over-empowers

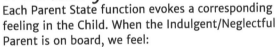

CHILD feelings

Each Parent State function evokes a corresponding feeling in the Child. When the Indulgent/Neglectful Parent is on board, we feel:

→ addicted → victimized
→ entitled → tantruming
→ selfish → grandiose
→ narcissistic → stubborn

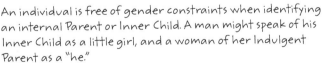

An individual is free of gender constraints when identifying an internal Parent or Inner Child. A man might speak of his Inner Child as a little girl, and a woman of her Indulgent Parent as a "he."

CASE STUDY:
The difficult task of identifying an INDULGENT PARENT

Julia, 25, was raised by two mothers. One, Eva, overly indulgent; and the other, Allison, constantly working to curb and buffer Eva's indulgence in which Julia revels. Everything was provided for. If she needed money, she would just ask Eva. If she needed a new car, just ask Eva. If she needed a vacation and a business class ticket, just ask Eva. Who could ever view being spoiled in this manner as a problem?

Julia's situation was even more complicated since she had learned to view her other mother, Allison, as a Critical Parent. Allison wanted to provide Julia with the rules, boundaries and limitations that she knew her partner was not invoking. As Allison tried to compensate for Eva's spoiling, she inevitably was seen as the enemy.

Addressing the Indulgent Parent is challenging. The Inner Child that has learned they can get everything they want seldom sees a need for change. Julia in fact came to therapy to address her difficult relationship with her "problem parent," the interfering Allison. Through her Inner Child work, Julia was able to see that in fact Eva's parenting style was the actual problem. She was able to peel back the layers of filtered experiences and see how each Parent Filter was impacting her Inner Child. She was able to identify the spoiled, tantruming, entitled Child within, and came to understand that if she were to re-parent herself, this parenting style had to stop. She had to listen to the voice of her little girl within, a voice that revealed she in fact wasn't happy with so little re-sponsibility over her own life. She wanted to learn how to exercise her potential.

INDULGENT/
NEGLECTFUL
PARENT

(P)
(A)
(C)

CASE STUDY:
Without a parent model, we can
indulge negative life stances

Here's **Evan**—age 32. He grew up hidden behind a curtain of drama. Evan's father had an affair with his wife's sister. This scandal was known all over the community. It was all anybody talked about. Evan's parents were so involved in their own drama that they neglected to care for their son. They failed to think of the repercussions of their situation on Evan. Instead he was left on his own to deal with community gossip. No one thought to ask him how this affair was impacting him. He found himself entirely neglected.

Evan had to adapt. He chose the adaptation of becoming a mean, aggressive boy. Nobody cared about him; why should he care about anybody else? He went through a string of relationships—all ending with women claiming he was abusive. Eventually Evan came to me because he had had enough. He was fighting his demons, but he was losing. He needed help.

Evan's adaptation was evident the moment he walked through the door. His energy was fiercely stating, "Nobody is going to get through to me and especially not you, Jacobs!"

Through my practice, I have grown to know these men well. I have learned they are frightened boys at the core, begging to be helped yet petrified of breaking down their stance of "I can handle this. There is nothing wrong!"

In Evan's case the Indulgent/Neglectful Parent had done its work. Evan's adaptations were set. But, instead of creating an entitled, spoiled, narcissistic child, it created a stance of, "You see, everybody will eventually hurt you. Keep people away; they can't be trusted." Evan indulged this way of thinking and filtered everything through that lens.

CATASTROPHIZING PARENT

This Parent gives in to *thoughts*, an approach which differs from the Indulgent/Neglectful Parent who gives in to *behaviours, beliefs* or *stances* (i.e. a position in life such as victimhood). The Catastrophizing Parent is constantly obsessing and ruminating about all the terrible things that can happen in life. Such a Parent is characterized by the

"What ifs,"

"Uh-ohs"

"OMGs"

This Parent filter torments the Child by inducing fear.

Anytime you hear yourself or anyone else say the following things, it is the Catastrophizing Parent:

 What if the plane crashes?

What if I don't get the job?

What if he/she doesn't call back?

Uh-oh, (insert name of daughter) she seems moody again today. What if her friends are ghosting her on social media?

OMG, he hardly studied for the exam. What if he doesn't do well?

Uh oh, I have a sore throat! I'm going to lose the whole week.

It's 3 a.m. and I can't get back to sleep. I'll never manage tomorrow at work. I have such a big day. I'll never get through it.

Uh-oh, you're in big trouble. She said she wants to speak to you later. Oh, no! What if it's about your job? What if it's about your comment last week?

You'll never be able to get through this. Never! What'll you do?? It's going to be awful!

OMG! It's my mother calling. What if she has fallen?

OMG, I just saw my partner glance at her/his texts. What if he/she is having an affair?

PARENT functions
The Catastrophizing Parent engages in a variety of functions, all of which impact the Inner Child. The Catastrophizing Parent:
→ frightens
→ immobilizes
→ overwhelms
→ paralyzes

CHILD feelings
Each Parent State function evokes a corresponding feeling in the Child. When the Catastrophizing Parent is on board, we feel:
→ anxious
→ needy
→ fearful
→ overwhelmed
→ paralyzed
→ helpless
→ paranoid/suspicious

When the Catastrophizing Parent renders a Child State fearful, needy or anxious, the Critical Parent often takes over in an attempt to control the situation.

CASE STUDY:
How we filter experiences impacts
our emotional responses

Let's meet **Claire.**

Claire is a 48-year-old woman, married and raising two daughters. She works a small clothing business out of her home three days a week. Her older daughter, Kayla, has a history of addictions and mental health issues. For the past two years, however, Kayla has been working hard on her rehab and therapy; she is showing no signs of relapse and is even attending school and doing well. Nonetheless Claire finds herself always on high alert regarding her daughter. At any and every moment, she expects to receive a phone call from one of her daughter's friends telling her of Kayla's relapse, or a phone call from the police informing her that Kayla is in trouble again. Her husband, Jim, however, is not as worried. Of course he is concerned, but he does not allow a Catastrophizing Parent to rule him. He has perspective from his Guide.

This case is the perfect example of how to tease out an external real circumstance from an internal filter system. True, that Claire's daughter has engaged in dangerous, unhealthy behaviours, and that Claire has had to manage the fall-out. The external circumstances are real. They alone cause Claire distress, as they would anyone.

On top of this difficult situation, however, sits Claire's filter system. She is always in her Catastrophizing Parent, riddled with the "What ifs," Uh-ohs" and "OMGs." So Claire, on her own, is adding intensity to the already existing external situation.

For example: The phone rings. Claire immediately goes into alarm mode. "What if it's Kayla and she's relapsed?" "Uh oh, the bank is calling. Maybe Kayla has stolen more money from us again?" "OMG, it's 2:00 a.m. and Kayla's not home yet." Claire is anxious all the time.

Now take Jim. He lives with the same situation. The external circumstances have not changed. Why is he not anxious and paralyzed every minute? Because his filter system is not catastrophizing. He has chosen a different way of managing the situation, which is by employing perspective from the Guide.

For example: The phone rings. Jim says, "I'll get the phone," or, "I wonder who's calling?" or, "It's 2:00 a.m. and Kayla's not home. No news is good news. Kayla has been stable for two years."

Where Claire is anxious all the time, Jim is not. We can see how our filter system plays a large role in how we feel.

If my happiness is dependent upon someone else changing, I will live in chronic dissatisfaction.

PROTECTIVE PARENT

The following parents are our three Healthy Parents.

PROTECTIVE PARENT

The Protective Parent comes to our rescue. It will move everything and everyone out of the way to protect its child. It is our "Mama/Papa Bear." The Protective Parent takes down the bully as its primary function is to apprehend the Unhealthy Parent State that is tormenting us.

The Protective Parent can take on the task of protecting us either from an actual external threat or from an internal Unhealthy Parent, or from both.

Anytime you hear yourself or anyone else say the following things, it is the Protective Parent:

66 *Hey, enough of that!*

Don't talk to him that way!

BACK OFF!

We're done with you.
You will not speak to her in that way!

Understanding this concept is often easier when it relates to protecting someone outside ourselves such as our children, our sibling, our friend or our partner. People are generally more protective of their own actual children or family members or their pets than they are of their own Inner Child state.

Your Child State encompasses ALL of your feelings. Anytime you FEEL, you are in your Child State and that is why we never lose this part of us. We FEEL until the end.

When I ask my clients what they would do if they witnessed their child surrounded by a group of peers who were mocking the child, laughing and jeering, even physically becoming aggressive, I hear remarks such as:

"I would bury them."

"I would take them down."

"I would step in and save my child."

I ask my clients what they would do if they saw a helpless animal being kicked by its owner, then witnessed the animal lying injured and whimpering. My clients respond with:

"I would attack the person."

"I would hurt the person."

"I would do anything to protect that animal."

Now I ask them what they do when their own internal voice is calling them "stupid" after making a mistake, or saying other hurtful things such as, "Nobody likes you anyway," or, "There are reasons you have no friends," or "There is nothing redeeming about you," and the response is usually,

"Nothing."

Too often we fail to enlist the support of this Protective Parent Filter who is capable of coming on board as a first line of defence when our Inner Child is feeling vulnerable.

PARENT functions

The Protective Parent engages in a variety of functions, all of which impact the Inner Child. The Protective Parent:

→ protects
→ shields
→ defends
→ saves

CHILD feelings

Each Parent State function evokes a corresponding feeling in the Child. When the Protective Parent is on board, we feel:

→ safe
→ protected
→ secure

(P)
(A)
(C)

CASE STUDY:
Protecting others can prove easier than protecting ourselves

Luke, age 35, had never learned to stand up for himself. He was bullied as a child by his father and was also bullied at school. His mother was anxious, and never stepped in to support him effectively. He had no one to model the Protective Parent. There was nobody who taught Luke how to protect himself. This became a theme in his life.

Luke walked through life unable to find his voice. He was focused on pleasing others and altering his behaviour so that people would like him. He morphed into a chameleon. He grew quiet and afraid.

Eventually Luke married and had two daughters. His oldest daughter was showing signs of fear and anxiety. She was having difficulty finding her voice. It turned out she was letting the kids at school push her around. Luke could see how she was being used by the "leader" of her peer group, how his daughter was being alternately accepted then tossed aside.

One day at a school skating party, Luke witnessed firsthand his daughter being bullied at the hands of the leader. Without hesitation, Luke marched over to the bully, and in a firm, loud voice said, "Enough of this! This has got to stop!"

This was Luke's Protective Parent stepping up to protect his actual child, something he had never been able to do for himself. This event proved to be an opening; Luke began learning to protect his own Inner Child. He finally recognized that he in fact had the skills, but had never applied them to his own little boy inside. Responding to his daughter's situation allowed him to see that he was ready to learn to protect himself by enlisting his Protective Parent. He was also modelling what it looked liked to stand up for yourself.

NURTURING PARENT

The Nurturing Parent cares for our emotional well-being. It makes us feel loved, cared for, validated, and leads to the happy, playful, fun and enthusiastic Child. The Nurturing Parent is always a soft place for our children and Inner Child to land. It wraps its warm arms around us and holds us close.

The Nurturing Parent has perfected what I call RAV—Recognition, Acknowledgment, Validation. This function is a hallmark sign of this healthy Parent, as it reflects the deep empathy that our Child State needs in order to complete the healing process.

Anytime you hear yourself or anyone else say the following things, it is the Nurturing Parent:

66 *I am here for you.*

Everything is going to be OK.

I can understand how you would feel so _____ (insert feeling).

That must have been terrible for you.

What can I do to make it better?

I'm not leaving you.

Look at me. Breathe!

You are a good, kind, thoughtful person.

A combination of family of origin story and inherent personality together shape how our Parent States filter experiences.

PARENT functions

The Nurturing Parent engages in a variety of functions, all of which impact the Inner Child. The Nurturing Parent:

→ nurtures   → cares for
→ reassures   → validates
→ soothes   → understands
→ comforts   → encourages
→ loves   → supports

CHILD feelings

Each Parent State function evokes a corresponding feeling in the Child. When the Nurturing Parent is on board, we feel:

→ happy   → free
→ playful   → passionate
→ loved   → sexual
→ funny   → adventurous

CASE STUDY:
When we can love ourselves

Meet **Lily**. Lily is 22-years-old and has been overweight most of her life. Her mother and father were both weight conscious and had subtle ways that could have made Lily feel badly about herself.

When Lily left the house, she might have had a complex about her weight and her body but she didn't. Why not? Because Lily had a strong innate Nurturing Parent who thought she was beautiful, smart, likeable and competent. After all, our filter system is partly imprinted through our family of origin story, and—luckily for Lily—is also in part embedded into our personality from birth. When Lily walked by a mirror, she didn't see the unworthy, fat girl her parents may have subtly been reflecting back at her. She saw a smart, capable woman. Lily's Nurturing Parent had been holding her Inner Child's hand, saying things like, "You are beautiful. You sure know how to get things done. People like you so much. You are so funny!" Lily's Guide was able to say, "Your parents' need for things to look a certain way is their need, it doesn't have to be yours. You've learned—through your own wisdom and despite your parents' teachings—that it's what is on the inside that really makes you who you are."

Lily was able to access her Nurturing Parent and Guide based on her personality and values. Despite who our parents are and what they teach us, we all possess an intuition of what feels right for us, providing we listen within.

GUIDE

We can think of the Guide, our third Healthy Parent State, as our "therapist"—the filter that instructs the Child State to make good decisions and explains why we should make them. The Guide puts the pieces together, and explains the consequences and motivation of decisions. It looks at our patterns and history. It brings in the knowledge of our family of origin, using it to shed light on our behaviour. When our Child State is out of control and leaning towards negative adaptations, the Guide sets rules, boundaries and limitations, and is able to show us how these can help us. The Guide can see a healthy way forward because it understands the past.

Anytime you hear yourself or anyone else say the following things, it is the Guide:

66 I remember the last time this happened, and you said the reason you made that decision was because you were frightened.

Going through life hating can only hurt you in the end.

Getting defensive is an attempt to hide a part of yourself that you might not want to acknowledge.

No, you are not having another drink.

By choosing not to do your homework, there will be consequences at school. I don't feel comfortable rewarding you with screen time.

You know when you argue with Sean, it reminds you of your father and you get scared and shut down. This is Sean in front of you and he has never raged or hit you like your father has.

Let's look at another way of processing why you didn't make the team.

GUIDE

PARENT functions

The Guide engages in a variety of functions, all of which impact the Inner Child. The Guide:

- → guides
- → teaches
- → mentors
- → provides perspective
- → shows patterns
- → analyses
- → sets rules, boundaries and limitations

CHILD feelings

Each Parent State function evokes a corresponding feeling in the Child. When the Guide is on board, we feel:

- → curious
- → wise
- → empowered
- → confident
- → creative
- → capable

CASE STUDY:
Being able to see perspective

Adrianna, age 29, grew up with two highly critical parents. They undermined her at every turn, with every decision she made. They criticized her for her choice of school, her profession, her partner. They criticized the way she was raising her children. Under their constant fire, she ought to have developed little, if no, self-esteem; instead Adrianna had a strong internal Guide who was able to help her develop a healthy perspective.

Her Guide was able to look at her parents and separate their unhappiness from her own. Despite the negative teachings of her parents, Adrianna could rely on her own personality and values to offer herself perspective. Her Guide would say to her, "Your parents are miserable. They lived disappointing lives and neither feels that they have accomplished what they had set out to do in life. Now, they are getting older and are feeling the weight of their unfulfilled dreams. They are projecting their disappointments onto you." Although still painful, with perspective, Adrianna could move forward feeling strong and unhampered by her parents' criticisms. She was fortunate enough to have a strong, innate internal Guide. Some of us intrinsically know how to be nurturing or guiding to others yet struggle to display that same consideration to ourselves.

THE PARENT–CHILD HANDSHAKE

UNHEALTHY PARENTS

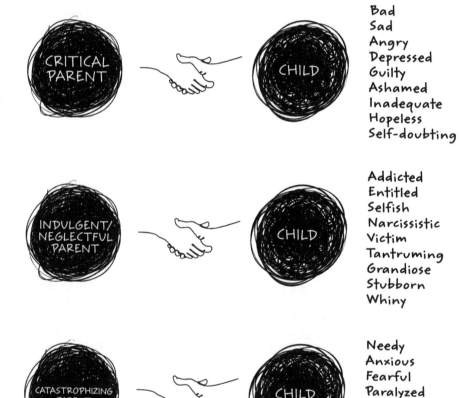

Bad
Sad
Angry
Depressed
Guilty
Ashamed
Inadequate
Hopeless
Self-doubting

Addicted
Entitled
Selfish
Narcissistic
Victim
Tantruming
Grandiose
Stubborn
Whiny

Needy
Anxious
Fearful
Paralyzed
Terrified
Immobilized
Helpless
Overwhelmed

HEALTHY PARENTS

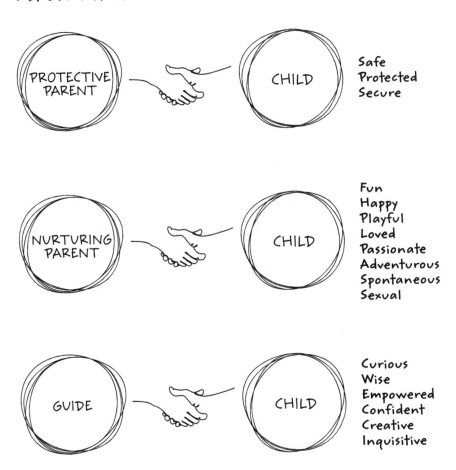

The Adult
(takes care of business)

The Adult State is relatively straightforward. This is the part of us that has learned to function in the world. It takes care of our life tasks, creating the framework within which we live. It is a place filled with decisions, actions and direction, fairly void of emotion. The Adult serves as the spokesperson for the Inner Child, able to express and act upon the Inner Child's feelings in a mature, unwounded manner. The Adult State continues to move things forward. The Adult State, like the Parent and Child States, also has a Healthy and an Unhealthy side.

HEALTHY ADULT
On the Healthy side, the Adult's functions include:

→ taking care of business
→ problem solving
→ making decisions
→ being rational and linear
→ having a conversation
→ explaining a reaction
→ being neutral

The Healthy Adult sounds like this:

66 *I have to be at work early tomorrow and, with the impending snowstorm, I think I'll set my alarm for an hour earlier.*

I won't have time to go out for lunch tomorrow. I guess I'll pack one so I won't be hungry.

I will now turn off my alarm and go take a shower.

I still have a lot of work to do and it's already late afternoon. I'll take my computer with me and work on the train on my way home. That way I can be less distracted by work tonight.

Oh my, the gas gauge is nearing empty. I'll go to the gas station and fill up.

It's time to pick up Max.

Hey Ms. Roberts, may I speak with you for a moment? I've been here for three years now and believe I have shown you my skills, expertise and value to your company. I'd like to discuss a raise.

Dan, yesterday when you compared me to my mother, I had a strong reaction and wanted to know what you actually meant.

I didn't appreciate that you just yelled at me for leaving the butter out, especially considering all the other things I have attended to today. And then you got mad because I said it hurt my feelings, and you walked away. I really need to know what was going on and I would like to discuss it.

UNHEALTHY ADULT

On the Unhealthy side, the Adult's functions include:

→ stonewalling
→ withdrawing
→ going behind the wall
→ being unavailable
→ shutting down

CASE STUDY:
What happens when your ADULT takes over?

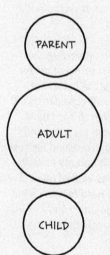

The diagram depicts someone who is primarily Adult, void of external emotion and taking care of business. This can play itself out in two different ways—from our Healthy and Unhealthy sides.

Working from the Healthy side of the Adult State, this person may be successful and viewed as reliable and dependable. This will be someone who will get the job done! Someone to count on.

Acting predominantly from the Unhealthy Side of the Adult State, this person may not be in touch with the feelings of their Inner Child. They may shut down emotion, and not allow themselves to feel. In this case, they can be perceived as hard to reach and difficult to read. They are challenging to reach emotionally. We refer to these people as being "behind the wall." The partner in this relationship is often left feeling lonely, isolated and not part of their relational world.

Too much self-sufficiency and independence can challenge relationships. When you let people help you, they feel purpose in your life.

(P)
(A) ## CASE STUDY:
(C) ## What happens when we
     ## hide behind the ADULT

Meet 52 year-old **Olivia**. An only child. Raised by a critical, abusive mother, and a "behind-the-wall" father. Olivia built her own wall, laying bricks to protect her Inner Child from the abuse.

All Olivia knew growing up was that whatever she did was not good enough. It didn't matter that she excelled in school, was captain of her volleyball team, was voted Prom Queen, and ran a chapter of Amnesty International. Nothing was good enough! Not only did Olivia's mother demean her, but she also physically abused her. Olivia walked on eggshells, as she never knew what would trigger her mother. Had she left her sweater on her chair at home? Did she put the glass in the dishwasher? Had she put away her folded laundry? Had she emptied all of the waste bins in the house?

Olivia was terrified all the time, never knowing what would lead to the next beating. The family was proud and private, and Olivia took note that she was never to share what was going on behind the closed doors of her home. She hid the bruises. She made excuses for her absences. She endured her pain silently. She silenced her little girl.

According to Olivia, her father was incapable of emotion. He didn't understand feelings and made sure never to discuss or acknowledge them. She said, "It was like living with a robot, a corpse. It was as if he didn't exist." And nothing, not bruises nor welts nor her mother's uncontrollable rages could get him to react or defend or protect her. He just retreated more.

By the time Olivia came to see me, she knew that she needed help. She had been married twice and was currently single, sharing custody of her two children with her second ex-husband. She couldn't make her relationships stick. She was beginning to see patterns, remembering feedback from others who had said she was not trusting and was difficult to get close to. She knew she had to let her guard down and let people in if she was going to develop intimate relationships. Understandably she couldn't chance letting people into her life and her heart. Her Critical Parent had convinced her of this. After all, people could turn on her; they might abuse her; they could rage on a dime. But, Olivia became committed to re-parenting her little girl; her journey is recounted in the chapter on Healing.

The Child State
(feels)

The Child is our heart and soul. It is our spirit, our spark, our energy. It is how we FEEL. How we feel about life, others, and about ourselves. Since we feel from the Child State, we never lose it or outgrow it. This Child State is directly related to the parents who raised us and how we continue to parent ourselves. Like our other States, this Child State has a positive and negative side. Whether we lean to one side or the other depends upon the way in which we were parented and the way in which we continue to parent ourselves. It is not surprising that the Child State sits at the centre of the Self-Integration Model.

Every person who comes for therapy is experiencing a wound in the Child State, in the place where they feel. People seek help for any one of a multitude of reasons. Perhaps they are upset, depressed, anxious, lost or afraid. Maybe they have just lost a parent, or have a child recently diagnosed with Autism Spectrum Disorder. Perhaps their partner has just left them, or they have few friends. They can't stop drinking, and alcohol is affecting their work life and relationships. They are addicted to porn or to sex. Or, maybe they cannot manage to stick to one job for longer than a year.

SIM asks us to identify the causes of the feelings evoked by these difficult circumstances. While we can often easily find an external trigger, we have to search deeper to perceive how we are filtering the experience and to understand the impact of this process on our lives. Our Filter, or Parent State, is what amplifies the distress we are feeling.

The Child State is a function of both how we were parented by our parents and also how we parent our child within.

CHILD

Our Child State is a very valuable part of us. It is where we feel our vitality, our ability to be playful, happy, fun, sexual. If our Inner Child is parented from the Healthy side of the model, we are on our way to becoming our best selves. If on the other hand our Inner Child is parented from the Unhealthy side, we will be prone to falling into any of the Unhealthy Child feeling States, such as depression, guilt, addiction, entitlement, anxiety or neediness to name a few.

In summary, the Parent-Child relationships will result in the following handshakes:

 If we were parented by the Critical Parent in our family of origin, our Inner Child will feel depressed, sad, bad, guilty, ashamed, hopeless, insecure, lacking in confidence, self-doubting, inadequate, unworthy.

 If we were parented by the Indulgent/ Neglectful Parent in our family of origin, our Inner Child will feel selfish, self-absorbed, entitled, addicted, whiny, narcissistic, tantruming, stubborn, self-pitying, victimized, grandiose.

 If we were parented by the Catastrophizing Parent in our family of origin, our Inner Child will feel needy fearful, helpless, paralyzed, immobilized, terrified.

 If we were parented by the Protective Parent in our family of origin, our Inner Child will feel safe and secure.

 If we were parented by the Nurturing Parent in our family of origin, our Inner Child will feel free, relaxed, fun, sexual, happy, playful, loved, passionate.

If we were parented by the Guide in our family of origin, our Inner Child will feel creative, curious, inquisitive, empowered, wise, confident, adventurous, able.

Our Inner Child will tell us what feels right despite who our parents are and what they have taught us. We just need to listen.

CASE STUDY:
When being caught in a Child State
can have negative consequences

Meet **Sabrina**, a 42-year-old woman. Sabrina enters the office, a glowing smile, big brown eyes, dressed in her workout clothes. She is married, in a childless, heterosexual relationship. She begins her family of origin story.

Sabrina and her older brother were raised by an entitled father, who did exactly what he wanted to do with little regard for his wife and children. His needs took precedence over the needs of everyone else. He lived on the edge, much like an adolescent boy. He flirted with danger, he gambled too much, he had affairs. He lived largely in his Child State—impulsive, unstable, selfish and entitled. Sabrina's father was incarcerated for an armed break and enter, causing enormous shame in the community. He was taken out of the home with little explanation to Sabrina and her brother. She could feel all eyes on her as she walked to school. She heard the whisperings from people in the neighbourhood. She tried to muster all she could from her resources and she pretended to be okay.

Her mother, who at this point was fed up with living with a husband who was such an out-of-control Child, left the family to create a new life for herself. Sabrina had no one. She and her brother, with whom she had little connection, went to live with an aunt who left Sabrina to fend for herself.

Sabrina had two parents absorbed in their own Child States with a brother who dealt with this trauma by going internal and behind the wall. Sabrina was left to manage the abandonment, neglect, anxiety and shame of her family situation. She had no one and had to figure out quickly how to manage this situation. As a result of Sabrina being raised by two parents in their Child States, she knew intuitively that if she were to survive, she would have to be the one to take care of business. She appeared on the outside to be the competent Adult.

Internally, Sabrina was in fact caught in her Child State, masquerading as a competent Adult fully in charge, yet with no ability to comfort, reassure or soothe herself. Sabrina looked as if she had it all together but was suffering inside. She had adapted. She was smart. She listened well, something she had learned to do as a child in order to anticipate her parent's next moves. She could have chosen many adaptations, such as acting out, experimenting with drugs and alcohol, becoming an overindulged Child herself. Instead she chose the adaptation of "I will make everything okay and take care of business." Inside, Sabrina was anxious and uncertain about everything. She didn't trust

A midlife crisis is when you realize that time is running out and you suddenly turn your attention to your previously neglected Inner Child.

herself and didn't trust others. She was playing a part. Her Catastrophizing Parent wouldn't loosen its grip. She was tormented by the *"What ifs, uh-ohs, and OMGs."* Her little girl was anxious and afraid.

Sabrina had a partner, but he was often away for work and expected Sabrina to manage his life at home. Meals were prepared, his travel itineraries were set, vacations were planned and bills were paid. Sabrina was doing what she was good at—taking care of business. Other than this support and occasional sex, her husband didn't demand much in the way of emotional care. She had chosen a safe partner for herself. Sabrina could have easily chosen a partner who resembled her parents' dominant Child States, but she felt too anxious with these kinds of men. She felt that the spontaneity and impulsivity could only lead to trouble. She had chosen security instead.

Sabrina became more and more depressed and lonely. She had difficulty maintaining relationships. The feedback from people was, "How come you know so much about me and I know so little about you?" "You always seem like you have it together," or, "You're such a good listener."

Sabrina knew she was on the edge, and needed help to learn how to be in the world in a different way. She wanted to leave behind her frightened, anticipatory Child State. She had never been parented by a Nurturing Parent or a Guide because she had no models of these roles; both her parents had been too absorbed in their own Child States. Her brother's adaptation had been to seal himself off and retreat behind the wall, so he was neither a place of comfort nor one of support. Sabrina came to therapy because she felt isolated, alone and distant from the world of relationships. She needed to learn how to parent her anxious Inner Child and lose the adaptation of "Superwoman."

Revisiting Adaptations

Our family of origin is the first place that teaches us about relationships. As children, we watch our families carefully, taking unconscious or even conscious notes about the dynamics that are being played out before us. Our family of origin is a powerful teaching tool; it will become the rehearsal for how we will deal with future relationships. Here is where we learn to rage, be silent, to become the comic relief, the scapegoat, the hero child, the entitled one, the fearful one.

We collect our feelings, reactions, and relational dynamics from our families. We carefully observe, making mental notes about how to behave or not behave in certain situations with certain people. In the family of origin most of us choose our way of behaving wisely, which we call our adaptation. What we fail to realize is that once we leave our family of origin, we can leave our adaptation behind... but, often we don't.

It is important to understand the meaning of adaptation. It is a change, or the process of change, by which one becomes better suited to a situation or environment.

We all live in families and learn to adapt to our surroundings. Let's take a family with a sad parent, for example. An adaptation for the child could be to become the clown, always making the sad parent laugh or smile. An angry parent? An adaptation could be to become silent and invisible to avoid becoming the target of this parent's rage. A troubled sibling? We could become the overachiever and golden child, never showing any flaws or needs.

We develop these ways of adapting, because we are smart. Most of the choices we make are based on the information we take in. The majority of these choices were wise choices in the family of origin based on the family dynamic. What then is the mistake we are making? We have loaded our knapsack full of adaptations based on our original family dynamic, and have carried this knapsack out into the world. Our error lies in how we continue to lug this knapsack around when these adaptations have often lost their relevance.

Let's take the example of the silent, invisible adaptation. Imagine that we have been brought up in a family where we have learned to stay behind the wall, not to draw attention to ourselves because that is what saved us in our family of origin. Now we are in the world and people are not all behaving as our parents did, yet we continue to behave in the same way. We use our old adaptations which are no longer relevant and end up being misplaced. We find ourselves lonely, isolated, disconnected from people. We notice that we don't have the same bonds that other people do. People don't seek us out, and we have no idea why. We know we are good inside, we mean well, we desire connection, but cannot figure out why it isn't happening.

The adaptations we used in our family of origin often do not serve us well any longer in our adult lives. What is the antidote? We need to become aware of the problem, understand the root of our chosen behaviour or reaction, and finally implement change. In other words, empty the knapsack and re-pack.

Holding on to old ill-suited behaviours and patterns doesn't help us move towards what is good for us nor help us move away from what is bad.

A VISUALIZATION:
Unpacking the knapsack

Imagine you have gathered all this information from your family of origin about how to react and behave. Now imagine having a knapsack and putting everything you have learned into that knapsack. By the time we are ready to leave our parental home, we pack our physical bags and we leave. What most of us don't realize is that strapped onto our backs is this heavy load we don't even know exists. We've carried it for so long that we do not even feel its weight. We've become familiar with it. We behave and react according to what's inside it. We are not even conscious of it.

What no one has told us is that at some point it is time to stop, remove the knapsack, unzip it, and pour the contents out for us to see. This deliberate un-packing gives us some distance and the accompanying objectivity to see what we have unconsciously been lugging around.

I like to think of this exercise as cleaning out our closet.

Once the contents have been spilled out, sort them into three possible piles:

1. **The KEEP pile.** This pile contains all things that continue to serve us well, get us to where we want to be, and fit with our values. These can be behaviours, thoughts and comments that we learned in our family of origin. Put these in the KEEP pile.

2. **The MODIFY pile.** These are things that have an essence of reasonability, but they are too strict, definite or inflexible. Take the essence of what you learned and modify it to fit your life and beliefs today. These understandings, beliefs and values likely come from your parents and may not fit with the person you have become. Put these in the MODIFY pile.

3. **The REJECT pile.** These are things that we realize have not served us well. Things that have no place in our lives today. The people in our lives are different and we have changed. They just don't fit, and no amount of modifying will change that. Put these in the REJECT pile.

Let me give you an example of each that was relevant to me:

1. **My KEEP pile.** I chose to keep a message from my father that taught me to be careful what you say about people. Growing up I am not sure I heard my father say anything negative about anyone. I am nowhere near what my father was, but I keep it as an important virtue.

2. **My MODIFY pile.** I chose to modify something my mother lived by. She thought it was important to be a positive energy. She liked to make people laugh. But along with that maxim was the message that people should not know when things are not going well. Keep smiling. Don't show anything negative or imperfect. I modified this. Yes, positive energy brings people closer, but it is also important to be human and to let down the happy façade when things are difficult. My belief is that close relationships are built on openness, sharing, vulnerability and support.

3. **My REJECT pile.** I remember being an impressionable eight year old. I was in the car with my parents and there was a teenage couple walking down the street with their arms around each other. I heard my mother say to my father; "That's disgusting. Those kids should know better than to be affectionate like that in public!" A few years later, during my own adolescence, I knew that this belonged in the REJECT pile.

Examining the Intensity of our Reactions

Life constantly provides us with situations that lead us to "feel." We all react. We react to events that occur in our lives, and to the way we interact with others. Our reaction depends upon the filter through which we have experienced the event. The intensity of our reaction will correspond to how the event triggered a wound in our core and the wound's place in our lived stories.

Let's play a game, a role play for a moment. You are at Starbucks and find yourself third in line. You are a little rushed for time. Just as you are nearing the counter, someone cuts in front of you. How do you react? Is it no big deal? You ignore it, and continue scrolling through social media on your phone? Or, do you kindly tap the person on the shoulder and inform them that the end of the line is behind you? Or, do you fume internally, but still keep silent? An angry dialogue burning in your head? Or, maybe you do explode, aggressively confronting the person who cut in front of you. Let's examine a few of the potential reactions you might have.

First case

You did nothing. Truly, you hardly noticed. Maybe you were distracted. Maybe forgiving. Maybe you were just not in a rush. You probably thought to yourself, "Obviously this person needs to cut in line. The five extra minutes won't make a difference in my life." This is your Guide filtering.

Second case

You redirected the person who jumped the line. You were coming from the Healthy side of your Adult State. You were taking care of business, dispensing information, and looking for a solution to the situation by directing the person to the end of the line.

Third case

You were angry but said nothing. Although you didn't actually show your reaction, you were instead experiencing an intense emotion internally. You have learned in life to be silent. You don't find your voice easily, and as a result allow other people's needs to surpass yours. Your wound has you place other people before yourself. Your reaction stems from your anxious Child.

Fourth case

You blew up. In this last response, your reaction was intense. I would bet your wound stems from having been overlooked in the family. Perhaps your needs were never important or met, or you were invisible in your family of origin, or always felt quite insignificant. Your reaction was caused by the Critical Parent.

As the reaction is more intense, the wound that is being triggered will trace back further into the family of origin story.

If we believe we have the ability to develop new adaptations after leaving our families of origin in order to meet the needs of our new life circumstances, we need to start by building an understanding of our wounds. We can explore the following process by examining first the feeling, second the behaviour or reaction, and third the wound. The accompanying worksheet helps us work through this process to uncover the theme or wound responsible for our related reactions and feelings.

The more intense the reaction, the longer or deeper the root or younger the wound.

THE MORE INTENSE THE REACTION, THE LONGER OR DEEPER THE ROOT OR YOUNGER THE WOUND

The SITUATION:

_____

_____

| REACTION |

Component 1
The FEELING:

_____

_____

_____

_____

— 50

— 40

Component 2
The BEHAVIOUR/REACTION:
(our adaptation)

_____

_____

_____

— 30

— 20

Component 3
The THEME/WOUND:

_____

_____

_____

_____

— 10

— 0

AGE

Back to our role play for a moment. Let's explore the fourth and most intense reaction, and use the accompanying worksheet to examine the roots of the feelings, the adaptation and the wound.

Please note that when doing this exercise, Component 1 (feeling) and Component 3 (theme/wound) are not the focus of change. The change comes from Component 2, by trying on new behaviours/reactions in order to change the old adaptation.

Component 1: FEELING

Ask yourself: How did I feel when that person cut in front of me?
Answer: I felt rage, anger!
Directive: Write this feeling under Component 1.

Component 2: BEHAVIOUR/REACTION = ADAPTATION

Ask yourself: When I feel that way in situations, how do I react?
Answer: I get in people's faces. I humiliate them.
Directive: Write this behaviour/reaction/adaptation under Component 2.

Component 3: WHAT IS THE THEME/WHAT IS MY WOUND?

Ask yourself: How far back do these feelings go? When do I first remember feeling this rage?
Answer: When I was a child, I would feel so angry that I would tantrum. I was always dismissed. People talked over me, no one cared about what I had to say or about my opinion, or my feelings or my tantrums. I was the youngest and I was invisible. I can remember that wound as young as age five. I became angry, a behaviour problem. Anyone who stepped in my way, I would make them see me.
Directive: Once you determine the onset of the wound, mark the age on the vertical age line. Identify the theme and mark it under Component 3.

We end up in therapy because we find we can't unpack our unhealthy reactions, which one way or another are having negative impacts on our lives. This worksheet helps us see the connection between our reaction in this moment today and the adaptation to our family of origin. The goal is to acknowledge our reaction, and to exchange the ineffective adaptation for one that suits our presently lived circumstances. We would like to heal the Inner Child, manage life from the Adult State and filter our experiences through the Healthy Parents.

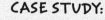

CASE STUDY:
Sam learns how his old adaptations
need updating

Sam is 68 years old and recently widowed. He has three children: Jacob (age 44), Sarah (age 42) and Ruth (age 39).

Sam comes to therapy because he has to make decisions about his will and is tormented about how to divvy up the estate without creating tension and conflict among his children. I can see the fear that is blocking him from reaching a decision. The intensity of the paralysis is worth looking at. We go in search of the depth of the root.

Component 1: FEELING
I ask Sam how he feels when he considers finalizing his will. He acknowledges that he feels paralyzed. When I push him to examine his helplessness, he waffles at first and skirts the topic of his children's behaviour, specifically of Sarah's. Eventually, it emerges that he is terrified of Sarah, his middle child.

Sarah has always frightened Sam. She is emotionally reactive, highly indulged and manipulative. She uses punishing tactics when she doesn't get what she wants, for example freezing him out for months and not allowing him access to his grandchildren. He says he knows by comments she has made that she has high expectations about his will. She has made it clear that, because her financial situation is less stable than those of her siblings, she feels entitled to a higher proportion of his estate. She has been asking her father what decisions he has made. Despite wanting to avoid any backlash, he knows he has to confront the situation. She is waiting for an answer.

Sam is feeling terrified.

Component 2: BEHAVIOUR/REACTION = ADAPTATION

I ask Sam how he behaves in the face of his fear. He explains that he walks on eggshells. He avoids the situation altogether by diverting conversations and evading his daughter's company.

Sam is avoidant and paralyzed.

Component 3: WHAT IS THE THEME/WHAT IS MY WOUND?

I ask Sam when he has felt this kind of fear before. When we explore his own family of origin story, Sam reveals that he too grew up in a family of three, and that his middle sister was highly indulged, highly reactive and highly emotional. Her instability had made him afraid. The whole family walked extra carefully around her, afraid of triggering an emotional tempest.

We see that just as Sam had avoided stepping on his sister's toes as a child, he and his wife avoided triggering their own daughter, similarly afraid of setting her off. They were frightened of the power that she had over them even when she was only a young child—or with later insight from therapy—the power that they had allowed her to have over them.

Next steps

Through therapy, Sam was able to see his frightened Inner Child whom he was parenting through his Catastrophizing Parent. He needed to enlist his 4 Healing Agents (Protective Parent, Nurturing Parent, Guide and Adult) in order to enable him to deal with his daughter's backlash, and stand up to her. He knew he was behaving like the frightened four-year-old from his family of origin. Nobody had taught him skills to say "no" or to deal with other people's bad behaviour or anger. Instead he had learned to flee discomfort, but now it was time to do things differently. He was ready to try on a new adaptation, and he knew his daughter wasn't going to like it. Still afraid, Sam enlisted his 4 Healing Agents to help him have the conversation he knew he needed to have with Sarah.

From his Adult State, Sam sat down with Sarah and said, "Sarah, I want to discuss my decision about my will with you. I have decided that I am going to divide the will equally between you three children. I know you may have a reaction to this, but I hope from the bottom of my heart, that you will accept my decision and continue having a relationship with me for the years I have left. If you choose to freeze me out, that is your decision, but I would hope that you can find another way to deal with your disappointment."

SAM'S WORKSHEET:
THE MORE INTENSE THE REACTION, THE LONGER OR DEEPER THE ROOT OR YOUNGER THE WOUND

The SITUATION:

Sam has to confront his
daughter about his will.

Component 1
The FEELING:

Anxious
Frightened
Terrified

Component 2
The BEHAVIOUR/REACTION:
(our adaptation)

Avoids
Puts it off

Component 3
The THEME/WOUND:

Speaking up will only lead to
disaster. Avoid conflict at all costs.

REACTION

- 50
- 40
- 30
- 20
- 10
- 0

AGE

CASE STUDY:
Isabelle develops a new adaptation
to an old wound

Let's meet 27-year-old **Isabelle**, a social worker on a palliative care unit. She is deeply disturbed by a young woman who is dying from an aggressive cancer. Her reaction to this woman is intense. She is crying at work, and not sleeping at night. Isabelle finds herself constantly obsessing about this woman, and tells me that there is no one at work to help her process this experience. No one with whom to debrief or share this loss.

While Isabelle's reaction is not completely uncommon, we know that there are many other professionals working with this young woman who are not as personally affected. So, what makes Isabelle's reaction so palpable?

We go looking for the root.

Component 1: FEELING
I ask Isabelle about how she feels on the ward. She tells me that she feels that nobody is there for her. There's nobody she can trust. Nobody with whom to debrief her fear.

She feels alone.

Component 2: BEHAVIOUR/REACTION = ADAPTATION
I ask Isabelle how she behaves when she feels this alone. She explains that, since she perceives no one to be there for her, she aims to process her feelings on her own. When she occasionally finds someone she thinks she can trust, she over-attaches and places an enormous amount of pressure on them.

Isabelle either shuts herself in, or attempts to rely heavily on someone else.

Component 3: WHAT IS THE THEME/WHAT IS MY WOUND?
I ask Isabelle to explore other times she has felt as alone with her feelings as she does now on the ward. Isabelle tells me of her early childhood. Up until the age of four, we realize that although her parents took care of her primary needs—food, shelter and clothing—her emotional needs were never met. No one had celebrated her when she achieved her milestones nor had anyone com-forted her in her failures. No one had taught her to self-soothe.

Isabelle's insecure attachment has made her very anxious. Her relationships as she was growing up—and even as an adult—had been fraught with anxiety.

She had never believed that people would be there for her, especially when she might have really needed them. At the age of 15, her fears had been further reinforced when she found out that both her parents were having extra-marital affairs. Her view of the world as an unsafe place was reinforced. Isabelle was certain that she couldn't count on people. People left. People let her down.

Next steps

Understanding the roots of her current feelings has offered Isabelle perspective. She is learning to accept her feelings since she cannot alter them, but to acknowledge that she can change the way she reacts to situations that trigger these old feelings. She does not need to respond as a 4-year-old nor as a 15-year-old. Instead, she realizes that she herself has the power to self-soothe, to seek companionship, to respond in a new way to an old trigger.

Isabelle has made the link between her intense present-day reaction and her past wound. In a pivotal moment, she realized that she is able to change her adaptation, which is based upon an old narrative.

Isabelle begins slowly. She gingerly experiments with opening up parts of herself to people she deems trustworthy. She is learning to self-soothe so that she doesn't need to burden everyone with every emotion. She is learning that by over-attaching to others, she is putting pressure on them. She is beginning to understand why people back away from her. She starts talking to others about her work and the associated sadness of working with some of her patients. Isabelle allows herself to share feelings and, in so doing, to lessen her burden.

Isabelle has learned to create a new adaptation for today of an old wound from yesteryear.

While we cannot change the sources of our wounds, we can alter how we react when they are triggered.

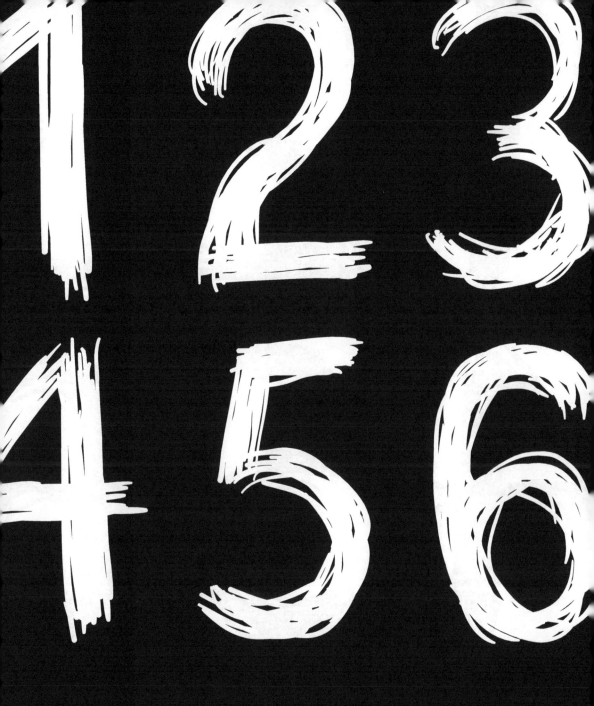

SECTION II

6 Step Healing
How we can learn to re-parent ourselves

The Self-Integration Model presents a six-step healing process that empowers us to alter how we respond to challenging situations. We learn how to filter lived experiences and how to act differently in difficult situations. We can choose how to react in the face of hard times. To apply the model successfully to our lives, we need to understand our family of origin so we can identify triggers and decipher adaptations. We also need to understand the roles of each of our 4 Healing Agents—the Protective Parent, the Nurturing Parent, the Guide and the Adult.

Armed with self-knowledge and a commitment to practice the model, we can manage our response to whatever life throws our way. The model asks us to follow these six steps, which will each be explained in greater detail in this second section of the book:

Step 1: Identify the FEELING + PULL THE ALARM

Step 2: Identify the UNHEALTHY PARENT on board

Step 3: Enlist the PROTECTIVE PARENT

Step 4: Enlist the NURTURING PARENT

Step 5: Enlist the GUIDE

Step 6: Enlist the ADULT

We are all equipped with the tools necessary to heal.

CASE STUDY:
Walk through the 6 steps with Daniel

Let's meet **Daniel**, age 37, who comes in for individual therapy. He has been working as a manager in a small business but doesn't feel acknowledged. He is not getting the recognition nor the raises that he feels he deserves. He knows he has become a behaviour problem—losing his temper, checking his personal cell phone on company time, talking behind people's backs. This adaptation, he knows, may cost him his job. Recently, his supervisor reprimanded him for coming in late again, and put a note in his file. Daniel is furious that he was being called out for what he sees as one bad behavior when none of his hard work elsewhere has been acknowledged. Notwithstanding his professional dis-appointment, Daniel is taken aback by his emotional reaction. "I can't believe the anger I feel inside," he says. We start there by exploring the intensity of the reaction by looking at the length and depth of the root.

It takes Daniel time and work to recognize what is behind his anger. When does Daniel first remember feeling this angry? He takes us back to his child-hood home at the age of seven. The house is filled with conflict—his parents are screaming, doors are slamming and swearing is abundant. His siblings are older and stay out at friends' houses most of the time. No one ever asks him how this rage is affecting him. It's as if nobody cares. Nobody listens to him, nobody hears him. He has no one to turn to and as a result begins to become a behavior problem—acting out, threatening to run away, slamming doors and breaking things.

We trace the root of his anger back to his family of origin where he felt alone, emotionally neglected, unheard, unimportant and invisible. Themes begin to emerge in Daniel's story. When do I count? What about me? When are my needs important? When do people care how I feel? When do they acknowledge and validate me? When do they make me feel as if I matter? He begins to realize the emotional neglect that he has lived with for years. As a result, instead of becoming the Critical Parent to himself, he becomes angry, and caught in self-pity. His Indulgent/Neglectful Parent is convincing him that he has a right to behave this way because of how mistreated he's been by everyone in his life. He is reacting from his "it's not fair, tantruming child." He is caught in a victim stance. Daniel needs to learn that if he keeps blaming others, this pattern will never change. Once he learns that he possesses the agency to change, his rela-tionships will change. He will be on the way to becoming his best self.

In any situation where he feels even mildly discounted, overlooked or invisible, Daniel reacts. Now after therapy he has the insight to know that the intensity of his reactions to day-to-day situations doesn't make sense. By tracing Daniel's reaction back to the beginning of the root we understand that he is communicating from his angry, neglected seven-year-old.

Daniel is learning through therapy, that in order to save his job, he needs to recognize that his anger is preventing him from responding appropriately and managing his behaviour more effectively. He is able to recognize that his Unhealthy Indulgent/Neglectful Parent has convinced him that the problem lies with everyone else, that he has the right to feel upset, and that he is justified in feeling indignant. He knows he has to re-parent little Daniel, not only to keep his job but also to change his parenting style with his own kids, to be kinder to his wife and to forge a new relationship with his parents.

Daniel will use the 6 steps to begin the healing process.

Step 1: Identify the FEELING + PULL THE ALARM

Anger. As soon as Daniel feels entitled to his anger, he knows his little boy inside needs help. By pulling the alarm, he is activating his 4 Healing Agents.

Step 2: Identify the UNHEALTHY PARENT on board

Indulgent/Neglectful Parent.

Step 3: Enlist the PROTECTIVE PARENT

Daniel knows he must enlist the Protective Parent (PP) who has already heard the alarm bell from Step 1, and knows its job is to STOP the Unhealthy Parent from fuelling the Inner Child's anger. Daniel is going to visualize the Protective Parent throwing the Indulgent/Neglectful Parent (I/N) into a soundproof room, effectively disabling it. As Daniel's PP slams the door closed, it will tell the I/N, "Enough of feeding Daniel this stuff. Making him believe he's entitled to be angry and defiant is no longer appropriate. Daniel can't hear you anymore; we're going to do this differently now."

Step 4: Enlist the NURTURING PARENT

This Healthy Parent has to validate Daniel's feelings, to reassure, comfort and soothe him.

1. "It must feel terrible to be working here for so long and be called out on being late while not getting any of the recognition you feel you deserve."
2. "It's going to be OK. I'm here with you. You're a good dedicated worker."
3. "Calm yourself. Let's breathe. Look at me. We've got this."

Step 5: Enlist the GUIDE

The Guide is important as it will chart the course forward, setting rules, boundaries and limitations. "Daniel, yes you have been working hard at your job despite being late recently. You feel you deserve more and your lack of engagement is a result of feeling underappreciated, but this is not your father, this is your boss. Taking responsibility for your lateness is a better option here since this pattern of behaviour is not serving you well. It's clouding over your other excellent work. How can we do better, Daniel?"

Step 6: Enlist the ADULT

"Since arriving on time for work is an ongoing issue, let's set out a new morning routine that will ensure we're on time. Clearly what you're doing is not effective. Nor is your anger helping. Instead let's email the supervisor so we can set up a time to have a larger conversation about your performance and engagement at work. We will go into his office and speak from our adult and not the seven-year-old. We can get through this; we don't need to get enraged and furious."

As Daniel takes himself through the six steps of healing, he can shake off the old adaptation of anger and entitlement, and instead recruit the four Healing Agents to carry him forward with a healthier response to the negative feelings he has towards work.

Re-parenting the Inner Child is work. We have to accept that it will take time, repetition, practice and commitment to learning new responses in the face of old triggers. Different tools and strategies can support us as we practise the model and develop new adaptations that will serve us better in our present lives. As we examine each of the steps more closely, the stories of my clients serve to illustrate how they begin to re-parent themselves.

STEP 1

Step 1:
Identify the Feeling + Pull the Alarm

Inevitably we feel the impact of challenging events on our lives. Depending upon which Parent State—or filter system—is on board, our Inner Child will either react positively or negatively.

Sometimes mundane circumstances cause unwarranted and over exaggerated negative responses. For example, when we overreact to heavy traffic, a bad call on the sports field or a misplaced item at home, an intense reaction might suggest that an old adaptation is being triggered.

Other times something terrible can happen that will shake us to our core. We might lose our job, discover infidelity or default on the mortgage. In these instances, it is natural to feel shock, insecurity, self-doubt, anger and a host of other difficult emotions. Independent of the life circumstance and accompanying emotional response, the Parent filters we apply to a situation add an entirely new dimension and intensity to our experience. We need to ask ourselves, "On a scale of 1 to 10, how much power does this external event have to impact the intensity of our reaction?" When our response rates the event much higher than warranted, we can acknowledge that it is our filter system impacting our response.

Once we recognize that our filter system is interfering with our external experience, we move on to examine the handshake that is governing our response. Identify the feeling—your response—and trace it back to your filter system to identify which Parent is on board. We must be able to recognize how our Inner Child is feeling to understand how we need to re-parent ourselves.

For some, a great deal of work has to be done to reach the Inner Child who has been hiding for years behind a wall of adaptations that perhaps were once useful but no longer are. Working to understand the family of origin can help a person gain insight into current feelings. The goal is to become more practised at identifying troublesome feelings that relate to wounds that run deep and are accompanied by inappropriate adaptations. We learn to complete Step 1 of the Healing Process in an instant, recognizing immediately when our Inner Child needs to be rescued. There are two worksheets at the end of this book and available for download at donnajacobs.ca, which can help you practise this Inner Child work.

When we recognize that the Inner Child is in trouble, we must call immediately for help. I ask people to pull the alarm bell so that their Inner Child doesn't stay mired in shame, entitlement or anxiety. As soon as we pull the alarm bell, we cue the next steps—we activate our 4 Healing Agents: the 3 Healthy Parents and our Adult.

CASE STUDY:
How Evan reached beyond anger to
find fear in his Inner Child

Remember **Evan?** Evan is the angry 32-year-old man who presented in my office with a fortifying wall around himself. He had learned to block out the world when he was a child facing the gossip of his father's scandalous affair. He grew up feeling like no one cared about him so he decided there was no reason he should care for anyone else. He had become mean and aggressive.

Evan's story is another example of how the Indulgent/Neglectful Parent works. But this time instead of creating an entitled, spoiled, narcissistic Child, this Parent creates a stance of, "Keep people away, they can't be trusted. Everyone will hurt you eventually." Evan indulged this way of thinking and filtered everything through that lens. He demonstrated anger, but was feeling afraid and lonely at his core.

We started slowly. He needed to trust me. We talked about his childhood and the impact of the affair between his father and his aunt. We spoke of the neglect he experienced as a result of the scandal. We discussed how he was raised by preoccupied parents who at the time were absorbed in their own crisis.

Evan was angry, and he was taking it out on the world. Anybody who got too close was a potential recipient of his rage. I knew I could be next. I knew I had to tread carefully and lovingly, but with strength and confidence. I knew I had to introduce him to the 11-year-old boy inside of him who was kicking, screaming and begging for someone to take him into their arms. But so many years of his adaptation made it difficult. He feared, "What if I give this up and I fall apart?" "What if I have nothing to replace this with?" "What if I end up even angrier?"

He had a good point. These were good questions. It is important to supply someone with skills before taking away an old malfunctioning adaptation. He agreed to do his Inner Child work. We did visualizations of his little boy so that Evan could reach him. These exercises are powerful because people are introduced to parts of themselves that they have buried, denied, or avoided.

Evan was asked to contact his little boy. I asked him to close his eyes, to look within himself until he could find him. When he felt he had made contact, I directed questions towards him, for example, "What is he wearing? Where is he? What does he look like?"

In the visualization, we slowly introduce Evan of today to little Evan. We direct a conversation between them. We ask Evan to ask little Evan how he is feeling? And why? We ask little Evan to tell his story, and we sit patiently using all the skills of the Protective Parent, the Nurturing Parent and the Guide to lovingly support him.

Evan learned to look past his anger to see the little boy inside of himself, and to acknowledge his feelings of fear, mistrust and loneliness. When he was feeling those emotions arise rather than disappearing behind the wall, he learned to pull the alarm to activate his 4 Healing Agents. As Evan learned to validate and integrate this little boy's feelings into his own life, he also began to tear down his wall and to build new adaptations to suit his new relationships.

STEP 1

CASE STUDY:
How vulnerability can be masked
by old adaptations

Meet **Julian**, age 28. Julian came to therapy because his partner, Craig, had just broken up with him. As Julian told the story of his grief, I couldn't help but notice his attitude. He blamed others, he put people down and he called them names. He took no responsibility whatsoever for his part in the break up. He was determined to maintain this stance throughout the first few sessions. Every topic he brought up was laced with a forked tongue. "This one was a moron. That one was stupid. That one was controlling." He had a litany of complaints, and he was never to blame. Everyone was beneath him. One might say that he was stuck in his Critical Parent.

My job? To gently point out his critical, judgmental nature and help him to a place of vulnerability. His protective shield was like armour. I had to tread carefully.

I asked him three questions that come from Terry Real's Relational Life Therapy Model, which includes Inner Child healing. The targeted behaviours in Julian's case were his blame, lack of insight, and impenetrability:

1. Who did this to you in your family of origin? In other words, who had Julian witnessed behaving like this to him?
2. Who did you see do this to someone else in your family of origin? In other words, who had Julian seen behaving this way to another member of his family?
3. Who did you do this to and no one stopped you? In other words, when have you tantrumed or shut down as an adaptation or way of behaving, and nobody stopped you.

He paused for a moment. The penny was dropping. He had never seen himself as a brash, critical, demeaning young man who felt he had to put others down, and assumed no accountability.

His first answer was quick and short, "My father," he said.

Donna (D): And what was it like to be on the receiving end of his criticism and litany of put-downs?

Julian (J): Awful.

D: What impact did it have on you?

STEP 1

J: I felt less than, not worthy, no good.

D: Tell me more about that.

J: Every chance he got, he would put me down. Nothing was ever good enough. It's almost as if he liked shaming me and got some perverse pleasure out of it. After all, I was just a little boy.

D: Yes, you were just a little boy.

J: It was funny though, not funny haha, but he didn't treat my sister like that. She never got the brunt of his shaming. I often wondered if somewhere down deep inside he knew I was gay.

D: You must have been curious and wondered, "Why me and not her?" Julian, will you let me help you?

J: Ok, but with what?

D: Let me be direct here. You have become your father. You have learned to seal yourself off from shame behind an impenetrable wall. There is a little boy behind that wall who was, and is, very hurt, probably not dissimilar to your father's little boy. You have chosen the only way you know how to defend yourself—by putting others down. What do you think of that?

J: (Pause) I never thought of that. You're saying that he was brutal to me, and I became brutal to others as a way to protect myself?

D: That is exactly what I'm saying. There is a little, vulnerable boy inside you who needs to be healed. He needs to be heard and to know that he is a wonderful little boy, just one who keeps people away to protect himself from people getting too close and hurting him. One who criticizes and blames others to keep them away. After all, if they were to come too close, maybe what his father had said about him was true, and if it were true, people may dislike him and shame him too.

(Julian had invested in an adaptation of NOBODY WILL GET CLOSE and kept people away by being untouchable.)

J: How can you help me?

D: I think it's time to contact your little guy and re-parent him. It means doing some closed-eyes visualizations and using the Self-Integration Model to re-parent him. Are you up for the task?

J: OK.

D: I want you to close your eyes and see if you can contact the little boy who was being criticized by his father. When you have him in your mind's eye, let me know.

J: I have him.

D: How old is he?

J: Five.

D: Can you describe him to me?

J: He's got blond hair and blue eyes and he's wearing jeans and a t-shirt with T-Rex on it.

D: And where is he and what is he doing?

J: He is sitting in his room crying.

D: Would you ask him if you can approach him?

J: OK.

D: What does he say?

J: He shrugs his shoulders and says okay.

D: OK, I want you to approach slowly and ask him if you can sit beside him.

J: (Nods)

STEP 1

D: Can you ask him how he feels and, if he answers, can you tell me what he says?

J: (Gets teary) He says he's feeling stupid for spilling his drink at dinner. He was at dinner talking about his new teacher and accidentally knocked over his juice.

D: And then what happened?

J: He says his father started yelling and calling him a moron, saying, "How stupid are you to spill a drink? You're 5-years-old, you should know better!" (Julian is crying)

D: What do you want to tell your little 5-year-old?

J: I want to tell him that he....

D: Just tell him.

J: You are not stupid and you are not a moron. You are just a little boy who was excited to tell your story about the teacher and how she commented on your t-shirt. And just because Dad says these things, it isn't true! You are just a little boy! A little boy who was excited.

D: Julian, are you ready to re-parent this little boy? To protect him from people like your father, to validate his story, to nurture, reassure and comfort him? And then guide him with perspective and good mentoring?

J: (He nods)

D: I will teach you how to do that. When you are ready, come back to this room and open your eyes.

Julian wasn't accustomed to feeling the vulnerability his little boy had felt. He had learned to cut those feelings off, to devalue them. Through the model's work, he learned instead to acknowledge the little boy's pain and to show him compassion. In valuing young Julian's feelings, Julian of today could accept these same feelings into his current life. If he could learn to accept them, he could then also learn to re-parent—to enlist his 4 Healing Agents to overcome the Unhealthy Parent and build new adaptations.

Step 2:
Identify the Unhealthy Parent on Board

We know that particular Parent filters evoke specific, related emotional responses in the Child. Consequently, once we have identified the feeling in a particular situation, we can point to which of the Unhealthy Parents is responsible for that emotion. The 4 Healing Agents will know with whom they are dealing and how to proceed.

Let's say, for example, you lose your job. If you are feeling you are a failure, you know your Critical Parent is on board. If you are feeling victimized and reviewing all the times that life has been unfair and that nothing ever works out for you, you know the Indulgent/Neglectful Parent is on board. If you are feeling entitled and find yourself saying, "How could anyone fire me!" you know your Indulgent/Neglectful Parent is still on board. If, on the other hand, you are feeling anxious and hear yourself saying that you will never find another job, you know your Catastrophizing Parent is on board. When any of these feelings are present—shame, indulgence, entitlement or anxiety—you know that your filter system is interfering with your ability to cope with this loss.

As soon as the Inner Child has pulled the alarm, it is our job to identify the Unhealthy Parent who is threatening us. Once we know who's on board, we can cue the next steps, awakening the 3 Healthy Parents and our Adult—our 4 Healing Agents.

STEP 2

(P)
(A)   ## CASE STUDY:
(C)   ## Angie learns to identify the
      ## Parent Filters

Meet **Angie**, age 21.

Angie was a sickly child. She had more illness in her 21 years than most. Through these illnesses, she developed a view of her life, "You see, only bad things happen to me!" And now everything is viewed through this lens. If Angie got a parking ticket, her immediate reaction was, "Of course I would get a ticket!" When Angie's roof started leaking after the heavy rain storm, she said, "Look at all the other houses that remained dry. I have to have the one roof that leaks." When Angie got a diagnosis of Irritable Bowel Syndrome (IBS), her reaction was, "Of course, it'd be me!"

You can see how Angie was locked in an indulgent stance. She believed, "Poor me, only bad things happen to me," and this was affecting her little girl inside. Her Inner Child didn't have a chance if Angie was going to filter life events through this lens. She would always feel a victim of life.

Angie was not keen on relinquishing this stance. After all, this is how she defined herself. She knew no other way. She agreed to try a new internal filter system when I reassured her that before we took this stance away, I would provide her with a new lens through which she would begin seeing her life. We used the Empty Chair technique to explore different ways of perceiving her situation.

EMPTY CHAIR

Angie sat facing an empty chair as we invited each of the six Parents to visit her. She was to listen to what each Parent had to say, and to note how her little girl felt in response.

First up: The CRITICAL PARENT (CP)

CP: You're so sickly. People are not going to want to be around you. You have nothing to offer anyone.

Donna: Angie, how does this parent make you feel?

Angie: I feel bad and hopeless.

Next: INDULGENT/NEGLECTFUL PARENT (I/N)

I/N: Of course, only bad things happen to you. Look at your life. You're sick.

Donna: Angie, how does this parent make you feel?

Angie: I feel self-pity.

Next: CATASTROPHIZING PARENT (CAT P)

Cat P: What if you never get better? Uh oh, is that a new pain?

Donna: Angie, how does this parent make you feel?

Angie: I feel anxious and helpless.

Enter the Healthy Parents.

First: PROTECTIVE PARENT (PP)

PP: Enough of this talk all of you. We've had it! From now on you have no access to Angie. Whatever you have to say, goes through me! You hear me?

Donna: Angie, how does this parent make you feel?

Angie: I feel protected, like someone has my back.

Next: NURTURING PARENT (NP)

NP: I know you are frightened. It's been a long haul. I'm here with you. I want you to close your eyes and just listen to the sound of my voice and breathe.

Donna: Angie, how does this parent make you feel?

STEP 2

Angie: I feel calm.

Finally: The GUIDE (G)

G: Actually, it's been two years since you've had a relapse. Last year at this time, you were training for a 10K run. I want you to see how the Indulgent/ Neglectful Parent puts you in this place. The truth is that although you were very sick in the first ten years of your life, you have been fairly healthy up until this recent diagnosis of IBS. Let's look at how you fought and got through those tough years, harness that grit, keep the perspective and take down the I/N Parent.

Donna: Angie, how does this parent make you feel?

Angie: I feel able and pumped!

As Angie learned to identify and distinguish between the different Parent Filters, she gained control over which ones she wanted present in her life. Angie was able to cue up the alarm bell when she would notice the Indulgent/Neglectful Parent intrude.

Step 3:
Enlist the Protective Parent

The Protective Parent jumps to protect the Inner Child as soon as the alarm bell is sounded. Sometimes we need protection from an external event, but most often we need safeguarding from our own Internal Parent or Filter system.

It is easy to imagine a parent jumping to a child's defence in the face of an external threat. Picture a young elementary school-aged child cowering in front of his teacher who is red-faced, gesturing and raising her voice. You see the child whimpering and crying, unable to defend himself. It's easy to imagine the parent swooping through the doorway to protect the child. What does the parent do? The clients I have asked respond differently in detail, but always with the same strong protective instinct. They say that they would:

"...step in instantly!"

"...rush over to stand between them."

"...holler at the teacher and tell her to stop as I rushed over."

"...yell, 'Stop!'"

Whatever the response, one can easily imagine protecting that small child in the face of a threatening adult. Yet we find it much more difficult to come to our own Inner Child's defence. We must strive to enlist our Protective Parent with the equivalent urgency.

When enlisting our Protective Parent to remove an Unhealthy Parent from our Inner Child we can use visual or metaphorical strategies.

PROTECTIVE PARENT

STEP 3

My clients over the years have come up with many creative images or metaphors that they use to remove the Unhealthy Parent, including some of the following:

→ Shoving the Unhealthy Parent out of the room and closing the door
→ Placing the Unhealthy Parent in a soundproof room
→ Gagging and handcuffing the Unhealthy Parent
→ Tackling and sitting on the Unhealthy Parent
→ Putting up a stop sign
→ Freezing the Unhealthy Parent
→ Macing the Unhealthy Parent
→ Or my personal favourite, getting the Unhealthy Parent in a headlock

We each need to come up with our own way of stopping the Unhealthy Parent from reaching our Inner Child. Once we have been able to run that interference, we are ready to enlist the support of the rest of our Healing Agents, calling next on the Nurturing Parent.

STEP 3

CASE STUDY:
Watch Ray learn to stand up for himself

Ray, age 49, has a brother-in-law, Mo, who is sarcastic and seems to love putting Ray down at every opportunity. Ray knows his brother-in-law has this tendency as he has seen him do it to others, but this dynamic is particularly pronounced in their relationship. For years Ray has gone silent telling himself, "Oh, he's probably just kidding," or, "He doesn't really mean it," or, "Ugh! What a jerk!"

Meanwhile Ray had been learning the model during his years of therapy. He had learned about his 4 Healing Agents, and he was ready to activate his Protective Parent. He knew he had to do this if he was ever going to feel good about himself again. He couldn't allow himself to be the butt of someone else's jokes any longer.

On a June day when the entire family was getting together to celebrate the graduation of Mo's son, the onslaught began. Mo was relentless in his jibes, looking for greater and greater laughs. This time, however, Ray was ready. Instead of laughing it off and saying nothing, Ray knew that he had to protect his Inner Child, Little Ray. He decided to stand up for himself. He knew he didn't need to tiptoe around his relationship with Mo; they weren't going to get any closer. He recognized that he didn't need to worry about making his sister uncomfortable; she had seen it going on for years and didn't seem to care. Ray finally understood that the only one who had anything at stake, the only one who had something to lose if he did nothing, was Little Ray. He finally stood up to Mo and said, "Enough!"

So, you may be wondering what happened after Ray's attempt to stand up for himself.

a. Did Mo back down?

b. Did he apologize?

c. Did he get aggressive?

d. Did he get silent?

e. Did he begin shaming Ray and get more sarcastic?

What's your guess? If your guess was "c" or "e" you are indeed correct.

STEP 3

Mo is not a guy who backs down easily nor does he tolerate being spoken to like that. No one corrects Mo nor tells him how to behave. He can dish it out, but he won't take it.

In fact, Mo reacted in a mocking, shaming way, for which we had prepared Ray. Ray knew that this would be a possibility, but also knew that he had to protect Little Ray inside.

Mo: Oh, look at the big man, telling me it's enough!

Ray: Mo, I get that you aren't used to me standing up for myself, but quite frankly I am tired of your pot shots and sarcastic comments at my expense. I would love you to stop, but if you won't then the least I can do is tell you that 'it's enough'.

Mo: What the hell's the matter with you man, I'm just joking? God, how sensitive are you?!

Ray: I get that you think you are joking, but it isn't funny. We are going to have to agree to disagree, because this could go on all night. So, for now, when you say things that make me feel uncomfortable, I'm going to speak up. Whether you stop or not is your choice and if this affects our future relationship, I'd be sorry about that, but I will accept it.

Mo: Man, you need help.

Ray: (walks away)

Mo will have the last word, because that's who Mo is. Ray knows this. The win for Ray is letting his Inner Child know that someone will stand up for him. It doesn't mean the abuse stops; it means that he is finally standing up for and protecting Little Ray.

Step 4:
Enlist the Nurturing Parent

The Nurturing Parent will step in to recognize, acknowledge and validate (RAV) the Inner Child's feelings. Its goal is to ensure that the Child feels reassured, soothed and comforted. It isn't to offer false assurances in the face of real challenges. In the face of loss, for example, the Child does not need to hear an untruth, that everything is fine, but is instead strengthened by hearing, "I'm here with you. This is hard. You are not alone."

Imagining who comforted us as a child or who comforts us now can help summon our Nurturing Parent. If we find that we have never had that person in our lives, we can create them. We can base our Nurturing Parent on a fictional character, a public figure, or an imagined individual who can stand by us. It's an internal voice telling us that we are not alone. Maybe the Nurturing Parent tells us:

"It must have been so shocking!"

"I can understand that you feel rejected and confused."

"It must hurt so much."

"I know you must be feeling badly about yourself."

"I'm right here beside you."

The validation, reassurance and comfort provided by this parent will eventually calm the Child down since it is difficult to feel badly about ourselves when someone is holding us close, offering us comfort. We can still feel badly about losing a job because that is hard.

STEP 4

We can't, however, allow ourselves to criticize our core as if we are fundamentally flawed. We can feel sad about losing someone we are close to. We shouldn't, however indulge the fatalistic feeling that we will forever be alone. We can worry that we have missed a credit card payment, but we can't catastrophize and assume we will never balance our budget again. The Nurturing Parent respects our difficult emotions by validating them and comforting us through them.

If we find our Child sinking again, juggling those negative reactions, we can be assured that an Unhealthy Parent is back on board. In this case, sound the alarm again and swing back to Step 1.

NURTURING
PARENT

STEP 4

CASE STUDY:
Emma learns to support her Inner Child

Remember **Emma**, age 44, who was raised by a Critical Parent, her father? Despite seeming to have the perfect life, she never felt she was good enough. She was always striving for more—not to fulfil her own ambitions or dreams, but to prove to her father that she had arrived. It was never enough. Emma had lost faith in herself, never believing she was good enough. She made a pact to never ever show her herself—and her perceived flaws—to the world. She had closed herself off. She was immensely unhappy.

Emma's husband had qualities similar to those of her father so she continued to apply the same old adaptations from her family of origin to her new marriage. Her shame grew. We have all heard the expression "We marry our unfinished business," which means when we have an unfinished wound from our childhood, we sometimes marry a partner with similar qualities or a partner who brings out similar reactions. In order for us to finish the work we need to address the original source. Emma was ready to do the work.

It was hard to reach Emma's little girl. I could see in our therapy sessions that Emma needed to know everything; she was too frightened to admit when she didn't know something. When a new therapeutic concept was introduced, Emma would reply, "I knew that." She didn't want to let anyone see past her wall. Even in my office where we were trying to carve out space for her little girl, she would present the smart, capable woman who needed to be taken seriously, even by me. Her shame was so deep that she did not feel safe exposing her true self.

With time and softening, Emma began to gain greater insight into her family of origin. She was able to make links and associations to see how toxic her father had been for her. She knew that she had to heal the wound from her father in order to create a strong place for herself and be the woman she was truly meant to be.

Emma accepted that she had to teach her Inner Child that she was not defined by her father. She had to hear from her little girl in order to know how to begin the re-parenting. Emma had to stop dismissing her and stop applying her own Critical Parent filter.

STEP 4

Through Inner Child work, Emma brought her 4 Healing Agents on board to meet little Emma. We had her visualize her little girl whom she imagined to be six years old. We asked the Healing Agents to take turns introducing themselves to Emma. Emma played each role.

Her Protective Parent said, "I will stand up against your father the next time he puts you down. I will bring you to safety and tell him he has no more access to you."

Her Nurturing Parent stepped in and said, "I think you are such a smart, fabulous, little girl. And I'm here for you and am not leaving your side. You are loveable and have so many people in your world who feel the same way about you as I do."

As Emma learned to re-parent her Inner Child, her little girl began slowly to trust and believe that Emma would be there to give her the protection, love, support and validation she so desperately craved. She learned it was okay to have flaws and embrace them. She did not need to be perfect. Emma was ready to take her little girl by the hand and give her all that she needed and deserved. She was ready to enlist the Guide to live a more integrated self where her Inner Child could step out from behind the wall.

Step 5:
Enlist the Guide

The Guide offers perspective, showing us patterns and making associations between events and feelings. This Parent helps us understand our feelings, their causes and consequences. It helps explain the impact of an external event on our emotional state, and uncovers how our Parent Filter perpetuates this impact.

CASE STUDY:
Olivia uses her Guide to overcome old adaptations and early trauma

Remember 52-year-old **Olivia** who had escaped her intolerable childhood by retreating from all emotional connections? She had suffered abuse from her mother that left her mistrustful of others. Her Catastrophizing Parent was always present to expose supposed dangers at every corner.

Olivia had been a most industrious little girl. She had known at a very young age that the only way out of her family was money. She had understood if she left the family early, she would be disowned and on her own. That had been their power over her, and her mother had taken every opportunity to remind her, threatening her with, "You'll never succeed without us!" "Don't think you can leave us so easily." Olivia, however, had known she needed to get out. She had spent four childhood summers setting up a lemonade stand. Half the proceeds were to go to Amnesty International and half to what she referred to as her "getting-the-hell-out-of-the-house" fund.

The Guide can see a healthy way forward because it understands the past.

GUIDE

STEP 5

She recounted the pivotal moment in her life when she had realized she needed to leave. On a Tuesday afternoon, 16-year-old Olivia had returned home from school to find the house filled with rage. Something was very wrong. "What did I do now?" she had wondered. "Did I forget to mail mom's letter?" Olivia had no clue. She could not even describe what she had seen when she had climbed the stairs to her room. It had been thoroughly trashed, precious items broken and everything in disarray. Her mother was standing in the middle of the room holding the plastic "My Little Pony" container with her lemonade money. Her mother was raging. Olivia had seen the blackness in her eyes and had known not to enter the room. She had understood not to utter a word. Olivia had known her mother's interpretation: she had betrayed the family by hiding her lemonade stand earnings. At that moment, Olivia had recognized that her life depended on getting out of the house.

Healing Olivia
Olivia had a lot to do before beginning to reassemble her life.
→ She had to learn the model.
→ She had to understand the impact of her family of origin.
→ She had to rethink and redevelop her notion of self, and not give power to her mother and father to define her.
→ She had to become aware of her adaptations and how they were affecting her life and relationships today.
→ She had to learn not to cut and paste her mother's face onto every relationship.
→ She had to heal herself from the abusive trauma.
→ She had to make contact with her traumatized Inner Child.
→ She had to re-parent herself—by protecting, nurturing and guiding her little girl.

Learning the Model and understanding her family of origin
Olivia was smart and quickly learned and absorbed the 6 Parent States. She was able to label her mother as a Critical Parent. She understood that her mother was operating out of a need to control her own out-of-control emotions. Meanwhile her father was an Indulgent/Neglectful Parent—ignoring his daughter's emotional needs and remaining behind the wall in the Adult State. Olivia saw that she too had opted to stay behind the wall as well.

Recognizing and assessing adaptations
Olivia was able to see her adaptation of becoming overly industrious, overly vigilant, walled off and self-sufficient. She was a smart little girl and these

childhood adaptations likely saved her life. Olivia needed them to survive throughout her childhood. This part of therapy is always challenging as people do not want to give up the adaptations that saved them. And rightly so. In order for someone to give up an adaptation, we need to put other skills in place first.

She began to recognize the links between her difficulties in relationships and previous marriages to her family of origin. She began to see patterns and signs, and remember feedback from others who said she was difficult to get close to and was not trusting. She knew she had to let her guard down and let people in if she was going to develop intimate relationships. Understandably, however, she felt she couldn't chance letting people into her life and her heart. After all, they might turn on her, they could abuse her, they could rage on a dime.

Meeting her Inner Child

We began slowly to introduce her to her little girl through closed-eye visualization. She was able to see herself as a four-year-old, with her straight hair and big, beautiful, dark eyes. She could see her little girl wearing a red and white gingham dress with white tights and white shoes sitting on the floor with a book in her lap. She introduced herself. As they made contact, Olivia was instructed—with Little Olivia's permission—to slowly sit down beside her.

Olivia said to her Inner Child, "I know you've been terrorized for years and there was no one there to protect you. I know you are afraid and mistrusting, and there is no reason for you to trust or believe me. But, I am here now. I may not yet know what I'm doing, but I am learning through therapy and with the help of Donna. I can assure you from the bottom of my heart that I will never hurt you physically, emotionally or mentally. I want to assure you that you can be the little girl you were meant to be—the free spirit, the carefree, playful, happy child that you were never allowed to be. You had to be a smart little girl to keep yourself alive, and now I am here to take over."

Learning to re-parent

As Olivia's therapy progressed, she learned the language of the Protective Parent, the Nurturing Parent and the Guide. She was able to connect with her Inner Child and create a safer space. Over time, little Olivia slowly began to trust.

She was able to see her mother's behaviour through a psychiatric lens. She read books on the topic. The books helped validate her experience, reactions and feelings. She realized that her parents did not do a good job of parenting her. Her mother had been abusive, and her father's adaptation to her mother had been to shut down and tip-toe around the trouble. We did not need to villainize them nor blame anyone. Instead Olivia looked with curiosity at the seeds of behaviour, seeking to understand them, and ready to give back to others their part. She was ready to change what was in her power to change. She was ready to have agency over her own life.

The process was slow and we moved gingerly. I can become theatrical in my sessions to prove a point. I can act out the different SIM states and change the intensity of my voice. At the beginning of Olivia's therapy I quickly realized that this unpredictability and change of voice could easily trigger Olivia into a trauma state. She would think that if I sounded like her mother in a similarly raised voice, maybe I too could harm her. As therapy progressed, we were able to use this dynamic as growth. The more she strengthened her core, the more successfully she could withstand my "theatrics." The more clearly she knew that I was Donna and not her mother and that I would not hurt her, the more carefully she learned to listen to her little girl's needs and wants. She learned to breathe. The more confidence she gained, the more she was able to differentiate others from her mother, even if at times they sounded or looked the same. Eventually, she learned to speak from the Adult State on behalf of her Inner Child.

Olivia works through steps 1-6 of the 6 step healing process

Olivia's ongoing work was to keep her wall down, to allow external triggers to impact her and to learn to filter these events from the Healthy side of the model.

Let's watch as Olivia does her work in an actual situation that she had to navigate:

Olivia was checking in to a hotel. She was in the lobby waiting for the concierge. To her left she began to pick up negative energy that was immediately triggering to her Inner Child. The guest at the desk beside her was frustrated and had begun to berate an attendant behind the counter. This situation posed little real threat to Olivia, but—because of her history—her Catastrophizing Parent had taken over:

"OMG, someone is out of control!"

"What's going to happen."

"Uh oh, he's now raising his voice still louder, truly yelling at the desk clerk."

"What if he comes at me?" What if he starts throwing things?"

All of this took place in a nanosecond. Olivia was already triggered, and in her terrorized little girl state. This time, however, she was ready to re-parent.

As soon as she heard him yelling, felt the fear and heard the voice of her Catastrophizing Parent, she rushed in to take care of her little girl. Something neither of her parents had ever done.

Working the Model

Step 1: She identified her feeling—TERROR—and pulled the alarm to activate her 4 Healing Agents.

Step 2: She identified the Unhealthy Parent on board as the Catastrophizing Parent.

Step 3: The Protective Parent came charging out of the gate to protect her not only against this unhinged man but also her Catastrophizing Parent. This work is done as a visualization. A protective shield around Olivia with the Protective Parent standing between Olivia and this man and her Unhealthy Parent. As her Protective Parent, she said, "I've got this. No one is going to touch Olivia. You'll have to go through me first!"

Step 4: The Nurturing Parent quickly came to Olivia's side and held her close, reassuring her with words like, "I'm here. Nothing bad is going to happen. I'm not leaving you. No one is going to hurt you. Look at me and breathe!"

Step 5: The Guide said, "Olivia sweetheart, you are being triggered by the old trauma. This is not your mother. We are all here with you and with our help we are going to lessen your reaction of terror. This man is not angry at you and he cannot hurt you."

Once her Inner Child was cared for, and the Guide had offered perspective on the situation, Olivia could move into the final Step of the Healing Process, having her Adult step up and move forward appropriately. Olivia stayed with her bags, waited for the man to leave and when she deemed it safe, she approached the counter.

Let's think back to Ray, afraid and anticipating that his brother-in-law Mo will begin berating him. Now let's imagine Ray visualizing walking into the family get-together with his frightened little boy safely surrounded by his 4 Healing Agents. The first three clear the path for the Adult to follow behind.

A VISUAL REPRESENTATION OF THE CHILD SURROUNDED BY THE 4 HEALING AGENTS

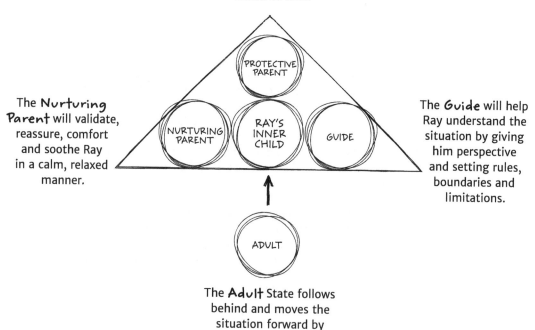

Ray's **Protective Parent** is positioned at the front, protecting him from Mo and his comments. It leads the way and keeps him out of harm's way by deflecting the onslaught. The Protective Parent will discard any Unhealthy Parent or actual external threat who tries to get access to him.

The **Nurturing Parent** will validate, reassure, comfort and soothe Ray in a calm, relaxed manner.

The **Guide** will help Ray understand the situation by giving him perspective and setting rules, boundaries and limitations.

The **Adult** State follows behind and moves the situation forward by taking care of business.

Ray's Inner Child flanked on either side by his Nurturing Parent and Guide, embedded with safe (protective), comforting (nurturing), smart (guide) parents who shield him from the toxicity of Mo.

Step 6:
Enlist the Adult

Our Adult State is able to take care of business. We bring this healing agent on board once the Child has been cared for and heard. The Adult is our Inner Child's voice, providing and executing the plan to move forward. The Adult can learn to discard old adaptations that are no longer relevant and develop new, healthier ones.

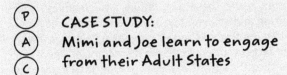

CASE STUDY:
Mimi and Joe learn to engage
from their Adult States

Mimi and **Joe** have been together for 20 years. Joe is 41; Mimi is 47.

They are committed to each other but continue to argue, armoured in their old adaptations.

Mimi gets nasty. She attacks, swears and is always on the offensive.

Joe retreats, gets silent and sulks.

I asked each of them Terry Real's three questions. These questions help identify the origins of these adaptations.

1. Who did this to you when you were younger?
2. Who did you watch do this to someone else when you were younger?
3. Who did you do this to and nobody stopped you?

Mimi replied that this aggressive behaviour is exactly how her mother fought when her mother felt hurt, upset, rejected.

Joe replied that his reaction mimics his mother's when she felt attacked or criticized.

The source of the adaptation identified enables us to tap into the Child State and ask:

→ When did this happen?
→ What did it feel like being the recipient?
→ When you were watching this unfold between your parents, how did it make you feel as an observer?
→ What were the results of these adaptations?

The next step was to take Mimi and Joe on a little journey for each of them to meet their respective Inner Child, and to characterize their fighting styles in a visual, much like a cartoon character.

Mimi described herself in these moments when fighting with Joe as a fiery little redhead, no more than 5 years of age, with pigtails all askew. She was wearing a red dress with red shoes and little bobby socks. Her face was all contorted and red as she tantrumed and attacked. This is how she learned to get what she thought she needed.

We called her—Little Miss Tantrum.

Joe, on the other hand, sees his little self as 4-years-old. He is dressed in a white shirt, black pants, horned-rimmed glasses with his hand out as a stop sign. We called him—Little Mr. Defensive.

I then asked them to envision sending these little four and five year olds into relationship with their partner, using these adaptations of screaming, yelling, attacking, silencing, pouting and sulking. I wanted them to see what they looked like objectively. I wanted Mimi to see herself jumping up and down with her pigtails flying and her red face. I wanted Joe to see his victimized "poor me" stance. I asked how effective they thought this was at getting what they truly wanted from their partner.

I then asked them, "What is it that you really want and need from your partner?"

Mimi: I just want to be considered. I just want Joe to validate me and see that I'm struggling. I want to feel part of a team.

Joe: I just want Mimi to see how hard I'm working. I need recognition that I'm trying really hard.

Donna to Mimi: How effective do you think your fiery red headed little girl is in getting her message across that she needs to feel considered?

Donna to Joe: How effective do you think your retreating four year old is in putting up a stop sign and withdrawing when all you want is Mimi to move closer?

Mimi and Joe were learning to take themselves through Steps 1 and 2 of the healing process. They were learning to pull the alarm when they identified the triggering feeling. They could identify the Unhealthy Parents they brought on board.

Mimi desperately wanted to be loved, but was pushing Joe away with her fiery little girl.

Joe was trying really hard, but not in the ways that Mimi desperately wanted.

In a closed-eyed visualization, I asked them to imagine standing face to face with their partner, while safely securing their Inner Children behind them. At this point, both Mimi and Joe were asked to draw on all 3 Healthy Parents in order to calm down the emotion and end with their Adult speaking on behalf of their wounded Child.

Step 3: Enlist the Protective Parent to protect
Step 4: Enlist the Nurturing Parent to validate and comfort
Step 5: Enlist the Guide to give perspective

We moved on to Step 6 of the Healing Process.

Step 6: Enlist the Adult to have an honest conversation on behalf of the Child about what they really need and why. Allow the Adult to speak on behalf of the child.

This is how the conversation unfolded:

Mimi: Joe, I was counting on you to finish the job you started. You said it would be done 2 days ago, and it's really hard for me to take care of the kids (ages 2 and 4) with paint, hammers and nails all around. It's hard for me to count on you when I feel let down. Can we talk about this?

Joe: I realize that this is so inconvenient for you and that you were counting on me and I let you down (Joe is practising RAV—Recognition, Acknowledgement and Validation). I over-promised because I was afraid that if I told you the truth about my timeline, you would get angry. I also see that in my being afraid of you, I overpromise and then let you down, which makes you feel angry and dismissed.

Mimi: Thank you for that. And, I know how hard you are working to provide for our family and I appreciate the stress that you are under. I just want us to be a team and if you're afraid of me, that doesn't help.

ADULT

STEP 6

Joe: I know being afraid of you only makes the problem worse. I guess I can speak from my fear next time and say, 'Mimi, I'm feeling anxious that I'm going to let you down, but I don't want to overpromise and I want you to know that I take seriously what you are asking. But realistically rushing home from work and cleaning up right away isn't going to work, so I don't want to promise you that.'

Donna: Ok guys, you've done a great job! Let's remember that fighting from your four and five year olds will NEVER get you closer to the secure attachment you are craving. The irony is that you both want the same thing— to get closer, to feel loved, supported and appreciated. So, let's put those little kids behind you, reassure them that they will be okay and step into the relationship from your Adult. Let the Adult maturely represent your Inner Child. Speak in terms of "we" so that you both keep the relationship team at the fore. I know it's a lot of work to have to deal with the emotion and simultaneously to understand the wound. Continuing your current dance is not an option as it will only make the work much harder in the long run.

The 6 Step Healing Process takes practice as we are working to alter behaviour that has shrouded the Inner Child since our family of origin beginnings. We can slip up at any stage as we work through the model. When we do, those old feelings will re-emerge. Now, however, with SIM in hand we are ready. When we falter, we will sound the alarm bell and head back to the start.

ADULT

STEP 6

CASE STUDY:
Accompany Vonnie through the 6 steps

Meet **Vonnie**. Vonnie is a 52-year-old woman, who came to therapy because everything made her anxious. One of Vonnie's two parents was extremely critical, while the other was always anxious. No one was there to help her find her way. She went through life afraid. She assumed everyone was judging her. As a result her Catastrophizing Parent was always on board waiting to be judged. She could not be comfortable in her own skin.

If she had a presentation at work, she worried that everyone was talking about her. When she made a decision to parent as a single mom, she assumed everyone was talking about her. When she bought her own condo, she worried that people were talking about her. When she received an email, she assumed the worst. When she got her hair cut, she assumed people were talking. It didn't end. She was plagued by a terrible internal filter system, the Catastrophizing Parent, that convinced her that people were judging her and talking about her.

All day long her internal monologue was saying things like:

"What if they think I'm stupid for suggesting that change?"

"OMG, she didn't say hello to me this morning. Did I do something wrong?"

"Uh oh, she's coming over to me. Maybe she's going to ask me about my decision to parent as a single mom."

"What if they think my condo is too expensive and are wondering where I got all that money."

Clearly Vonnie's Catastrophizing Parent had its grips on her. She was constantly tormented by this filter system and had to learn to re-parent herself from the healthy side of the model.

Vonnie was asked to do the 6 Step Healing process regularly. Anytime she heard that terrible voice, she was to perform her 6 Steps in order to activate her 4 Healing Agents—her Protective Parent, Nurturing Parent, Guide, and Adult.

Step 1: Identify the FEELING + PULL THE ALARM
Vonnie has just contributed to a discussion at a meeting and no one responded to her input. She immediately hears herself wondering whether her comment was irrelevant and dumb. She recognizes she is feeling anxious that people are judging her as stupid. Vonnie pulls the alarm.

STEP 6

Step 2: Identify the UNHEALTHY PARENT on board
Vonnie can recognize her Catastrophizing Parent immediately. All the work she has done in therapy and her ongoing practice is making it easier and easier for Vonnie to identify this Unhealthy Parent.

Step 3: Enlist the PROTECTIVE PARENT
The Protective Parent immediately goes to her aid. In a visualization, Vonnie's Protective Parent would step in between her little girl and the Catastrophizing Parent, stopping the latter in its tracks. If she had to get more physical in her visualization, she could use any of a number of images to see the intervention: a tackle, a head hold, a gagging rag.

Step 4: Enlist the NURTURING PARENT
Once the threat of the Catastrophizing Parent is gone, the Nurturing Parent moves in. She validates how terrible it must feel always to have this worry and anxiety caused by the Catastrophizing Parent. Then the Nurturing Parent holds Vonnie close and reassures her, telling her it will be okay. It says things like, " You are a wonderful woman and a smart woman. I think you have a lot to offer, and I'm here for you." Once Vonnie begins to calm down and feels the strength of her Nurturing Parent's arms around her, enter the Guide.

Step 5: Enter GUIDE
The Guide's job is to give perspective, to analyse, to teach. It tells Vonnie such things as,"Look at your life and how you've taken charge of it. Many people could not do what you've done. You know you were raised by an anxious parent and a critical parent who never taught you to self-soothe. And please know that everyone is too busy getting through their own lives to worry about yours. Yes, people might not have heard you this time, but that's okay. You know that it's a busy meeting and everyone is preoccupied. If your comment was important, you will find another opening to make sure it is heard."

Step 6: The ADULT
Finally the Adult steps in. The Adult's job is to take care of any business that is left hanging. The Adult might have her follow up from the meeting with an email if she thinks her contribution still needs to be heard. The Adult also might have her write a supportive letter to herself from her Nurturing Parent. It might suggest calling a friend to boost her up. The Adult helps Vonnie move forward in a healthy, constructive way.

STEP 6

As Vonnie learns to apply SIM to her own life, she begins to listen to her Inner Child, and enlists her Healing Agents to move forward in the Adult State. She feels comforted, secure and understands from her Guide what she needs. Like those in the stories this book has shared, if we commit to the work, SIM can give each of us a path forward towards more fulfilled lives. We can learn to alter our adaptations and to respond healthily to our lived circumstances. To do this work, however, we need to gain insight into our personal histories, our wounds and triggers. Sometimes we can gain this knowledge of ourselves through independent introspection. Sometimes we may need the help of a therapist to see the themes that govern our feelings and many of our interactions with others.

What is certain is that, as we practise SIM, we are well on our way to becoming our best selves.

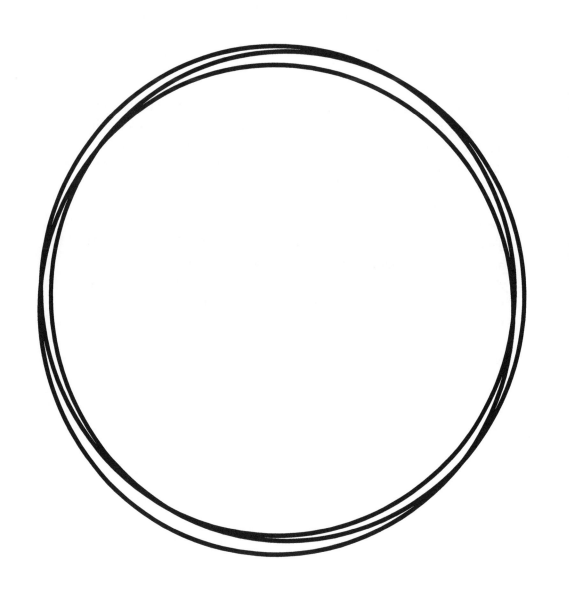

Conclusion

Where my road map has taken me

Our greatest creativity comes from personal experience. And in this case, this book is no different. The Self-Integration Model (SIM) was born from a part of me held in the grips of anxiety. It was from this personal experience and then meeting the personal experiences of thousands of others that I began to see that how we feel is largely dictated by something we possess internally—our Parent States or our Filter System. I thought if we possess the ability to make ourselves feel bad, angry, inadequate, guilty, entitled, anxious, needy and fearful, then we must have the ability to make ourselves feel happy, confident, loved, secure, enthusiastic and joyful as well.

Life hands us a myriad of challenges and of course these external events have an impact on how we feel. However, I maintain that the external situation is aggravated by how we filter these externals. Each ensuing feeling will be dependent upon which of the 6 lenses we choose. So, when I ask clients, "How do you want to do cancer/divorce/unemployment, etc?" I respectfully mean that there are six ways. We can do it angrily, victimized, or anxiously from the Unhealthy side of the model, or we can filter and parent ourselves through the Healthy side of the model—and feel secure, loved and empowered. The Self-Integration Model's goal is to integrate the healthy parts of self, re-parent ourselves and heal the Inner Child in the hopes that we are becoming our best selves.

I asked my Inner Child (my 13 year old) how she felt about the book and she said that she was really happy. I also asked her, "How different are we today?" My 13 year old of the past acknowledged that back then she felt lost. She didn't have a sense of her "true" self. She was focused on what others needed, never bothering to find out what she wanted or needed. She was afraid. She was anxious. She became a pleaser, then a "hippy"—still trying to find her way. This acknowledgment of her growth over the years has filled her with pride, empowerment and confidence. With hindsight, she can truly celebrate the gains she has made.

The irony was that this sense of being lost and the anxiety I felt ultimately led me to psychology and to the development of this model. And by virtue of this journey, I was able to spend years helping myself and others. And even further, hopefully leave a legacy of how we can re-parent ourselves out of early adaptations. Today, Donna's little girl would say, "I feel free! Free to be who I am. And free to allow others to be who they are. I feel confident and empowered."

I thank my Protective Parent for standing by me and letting me know that there is a shield for me if I run into danger, that someone has my back. I thank my Nurturing Parent for the validation, reassurance and soothing; for telling me I'm not alone and that we will get through this together. I thank my Guide for its wisdom and perspective; for helping me to see that being controlled by my Catastrophizing Parent will only lead to anxiety and helplessness; for reminding me that whatever was making me anxious always seems to turn to dust somewhere in the future. And I thank my Adult for taking care of business and moving forward; for always working to figure things out; for being a particularly good representative for my Child State. I thank her for knowing how to have a conversation on my Child's behalf and for staying in relationship with others.

Do I trip up? Yes.

Is it perfect? No.

But I have a map to becoming my best self and that's worth a lot. I wish you each strength in working on **becoming your best self.**

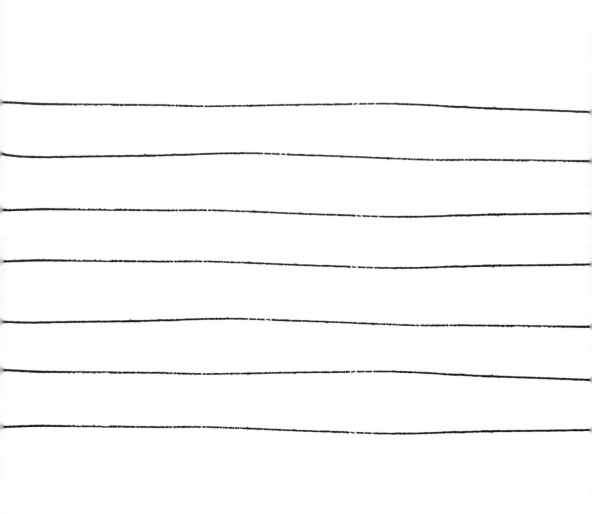

Worksheets

*For more resources and to download these worksheets, visit **donnajacobs.ca**.*

WORKSHEET:
GENERATIONS OF PAC

Use this worksheet to explore the PAC structure of those who impacted you, and to draw your own PAC.

Draw the PAC models for your parents or the people who raised you. Each parent would have three circles, of differing sizes, the larger circle representing the predominant state and the smallest the least dominant state.

Draw your own PAC with your predominant state largest, your more dormant state smallest.

Now add the *handshake*. Draw an arrow on your PAC (above) from your predominant Parent filter to your corresponding Child feelings. (Refer to pp. 30 and 56 for a summary of *handshakes*).

WORKSHEET:
6 STEP HEALING

Today's date:

The SITUATION:

On a scale from 0 to 10, rank the power that the external situation should have on making you distressed and upset (ie; *before* you filter it through an Unhealthy Parent).

Now rank on a scale from 0 to 10 your distress *after* your filter distorts it to see how much the Filter System is contributing to your feeling.

Step 1: Identify the feeling in the CHILD STATE
☐ Sad, angry, irritated, lonely, depressed, bad, inadequate, shamed, guilty, or
☐ Entitled, addicted, selfish, self-absorbed, whiny, victim, grandiose, or
☐ Anxious, fearful, stressed, helpless, immobilized

Pull the alarm to activate and engage the 4 Healing Agents

Step 2: Identify the UNHEALTHY PARENT on board
- ☐ Critical Parent ➔ All about control (criticize, judge, blame, punish)
- ☐ Indulgent/Neglectful Parent ➔ Giving in to behaviours/stances (addictions, entitlement, self-pity, tantrums)
- ☐ Catastrophizing Parent ➔ Giving in to thoughts (what ifs, uh ohs, OMGs)

ENLIST THE 4 HEALING AGENTS

Step 3: Enlist the PROTECTIVE PARENT
Bring the child to safety while apprehending the Unhealthy Parent on board. Use visualization to take down the Unhealthy Parent.

Step 4: Enlist the NURTURING PARENT
Validate, Reassure, Comfort:
1. Validation ➔ I know... this sucks, your heart is broken, you feel sad/angry/irritated
2. Reassurance: You, I, we language
   ➔ You are smart, funny, hard working
   ➔ I've got you, It's going to be okay, I've got your back
   ➔ We will get through this, we will be okay, we can do this
3. Comfort/Soothe: I am here, it's ok. Look at me. Breathe.

Step 5: Enlist the GUIDE ("the insightful therapist")
➔ Put the setback in context
➔ Point out the positive
➔ Understand the triggers
➔ Set rules, boundaries, limitations
➔ Analyze the pattern

Step 6: Enlist the ADULT
➔ Make a plan
➔ Take care of business
➔ Have a conversation

WORKSHEET:
THE MORE INTENSE THE REACTION,
THE LONGER OR DEEPER THE ROOT
OR YOUNGER THE WOUND

The SITUATION:

_____

_____

```
┌─────────────────┐
│    REACTION     │
└─────────────────┘
```

Component 1
The FEELING:

— 50

— 40

Component 2
The BEHAVIOUR/REACTION:
(our adaptation)

— 30

— 20

Component 3
The THEME/WOUND:

— 10

— 0

AGE

WORKSHEET:
MORNING CHECK-IN WITH YOUR INNER CHILD

This exercise is to be done in the morning. The purpose is to check in with our Inner Child to ensure that our Parent State is listening to know how we feel and to provide us with what we need and want.

1. "_____, (insert your name or nickname) How are you feeling?" (Ask yourself how you feel)

2. "Why are you feeling that way?" (Explain the situation that has contributed to the way you are feeling)

3. What do you need? What do you want? What can I do for you? What do you need me to do for you? What do you need or want from me now? Today?

These questions are addressed to the Child from the Healthy Parent State. Choose whichever question(s) fits for the moment. The goal is to provide something now for the child eg. a hug, a cup of tea, send an email, go for a walk, have a conversation with someone, etc. The idea is not to wish for change in the other person.

Adapted from Leonard Shaw's Inner Child work

WORKSHEET:
EVENING CHECK-IN WITH YOUR INNER CHILD

This exercise is to be done before bed. The purpose is to check in with our Inner Child to demonstrate how well our Parent State has listened, followed through and committed to us.

1. "_____, (insert your name or nickname) How are you feeling?" (Ask yourself how you feel)

2. "Why are you feeling that way?" (Explain the situation that has contributed to the way you feel)

3. How did I do today? Where did I listen to you? Where did I let you down? (This question gives the Child an opportunity to evaluate how well the Parent State did)

4. My commitment for tomorrow. (This is for the Healthy Parent to assess its strengths and weaknesses in caring for the Inner Child State and state a new commitment)

Adapted from Leonard Shaw's Inner Child work

Glossary

4 Healing Agents

Consists of the 3 Healthy Parents (Protective, Nurturing and Guide) and the Adult.

6 Step Healing

Process by which we identify a problematic feeling and the related Unhealthy Parent on board, and heal by moving to the Healthy side of the Model.

adaptation

Any behaviour or reaction that an individual develops in response to the dynamics of their family of origin.

Adult State

The part of us that deals with everyday life, by taking care of business and moving us forward.

agency

The ability of an individual to chart their own course and/or evoke change in their life.

Catastrophizing Parent

One of our 3 Unhealthy Parent States. The Parent State that gives in to thoughts and frightens us with all of the bad things that can happen.

Child State

Our internal place of feeling and the place we house our needs and wants.

Critical Parent

One of our 3 Unhealthy Parents States. The Parent State that judges and demeans us or others.

ego states
Conscious parts of us that possess consistent patterns of thinking, feeling and behaviour.

family of origin
Refers to the significant caretakers and family members with whom a person grows up.

filter system
The way an individual chooses to see, interpret and process any external event.

Guide
One of our 3 Healthy Parent States. The Parent State that offers perspective and insight into our feelings and motivations.

id
Freud's concept where our basic needs and instinctual drives reside.

Indulgent/Neglectful Parent
One of our 3 Unhealthy Parent States. The Parent State that gives in to behaviours, beliefs or a stance.

Inner Child
The repository of feelings in our psyche and the place of our emotional response.

Nurturing Parent
One of our 3 Healthy Parent States. The Parent State that holds us close, validates, comforts, soothes and reassures.

PAC
Parent, Adult, Child State.

Parent State

A parent state is the part of us that filters external situations and as a result causes our Child state to feel a certain way. We have 3 Healthy Parent States and 3 Unhealthy Parent States.

persona

A role or character that someone plays.

Protective Parent

One of our 3 Healthy Parent States. The Parent State that looks out for us and has our back.

psychodynamic

An approach to psychology that takes into account a person's unconscious drives and motivations.

R A V (©Donna Jacobs)

Recognition, Acknowledgment, Validation. Recognition—non verbally recognizing the other through eye contact, gestures, non verbal responses, attending behaviours to demonstrate that someone is present and has something to say. Acknowledgment—taking in, listening and hearing the content of what the person has to say. Validation—is the output. Understanding the corresponding feeling state that matched the other's words and empathically giving this back to the person.

re-parent

Refers to re-doing any unhealthy parenting that we were exposed to in our family of origin by bringing on our own Healthy Parents to heal us from past hurt.

Self-Integration

Taking the best parts of yourself from the Healthy side of the model and identifying your own thoughts, feelings, preferences and beliefs regardless of external influences.

stance
Positioning in the face of life dictated by a set of beliefs.

the Self
A term explored extensively in psychology in reference to the core of our being that distinguishes us from others, which Donna states is made up of our needs, wants, feelings, likes, dislikes, thoughts, beliefs and values.

theme
A recurring pattern of feelings, sensations or behaviours.

Transactional Analysis
Eric Berne's psychological theory which analyzes social interactions based on our different parts of self—Parent Adult Child.

trigger
Any stimulus that reminds us of an earlier event that was unpleasant.

wound
A psychological concept referring to an internal place where we have been hurt or damaged.

BIBLIOGRAPHY

Why Can't I Ever be Good Enough
Joan Rubin-Deutsch

Healing Your Emotional Self
Beverly Engel

What Your Mother Never Told You About Love, Sex and Power
Shelley Pomerantz and Mardi Thomas Goodman

The Four Agreements
Don Miguel Ruiz

I Don't Want to Talk About It
Terry Real

Daring Greatly
Brené Brown

Love and Forgiveness
Leonard Shaw

Healing the Child Within
Charles Whitfield

I'm OK You're OK
Thomas A. Harris

Games People Play
Eric Berne

Born To Win
James & Jongeward

ABOUT THE AUTHORS

Donna Jacobs is a clinical Psychologist who has been in practice for 40 years seeing individuals and couples. Throughout her professional career Donna has been exposed to many influences which have all helped shape and hone her therapy and her "Self-Integration Model."

Donna is excited to go to work every day and is grateful for her many clients, both past and present, who have instilled their trust in her. She believes that therapy (which can be difficult and painful) at its best is a process balancing creativity and excitement with insight and analysis.

Donna believes that when people identify the various parts of themselves, they can transform themselves to live happy, healthy and complete lives by becoming their best selves.

Donna has also worked extensively in the field of fertility, helping individuals and couples navigate the complicated, painful road of infertility. She has been a consultant to many of the fertility clinics in the city of Toronto.

Donna taught for many years at Concordia University in Montreal before making her move to Toronto in 1997 and was part of an online course on third party reproduction through TAPE studies for professionals in affiliation with St. Michael's College in the University of Toronto.

She has presented at conferences and for professional development and has had numerous television and radio appearances dealing with related topics to her practice. You may have seen Donna as a regular guest expert on City Line Television with Marilyn Dennis.

Donna's book is a creative endeavour, much like most of her life. Prior to Psychology, she completed a Fine arts degree which led to 18 years teaching in the Graduate Art Therapy Program at Concordia University while still maintaining her private practice.

Over 35 years Donna has sung professionally in various bands and has performed in many musical theatre productions.

This book of Donna's therapeutic model is a culmination of her 40 years in practice and her "Becoming Your Best Self" workshops, which are a wonderful blend of her two passions—Psychology and Performance. Donna lives in Toronto, Ontario with her husband, Steve, of 43 years and their 11-year-old Golden Doodle, Maggie. Donna and Steve are fortunate to have their two daughters, son-in-law, and three grandchildren living in close proximity to Toronto.

Sara Gardner completed both her undergraduate and post-graduate studies at the University of Toronto where she pursued a particular interest in the intersections of story and history. She went on to obtain her Bachelor of Education from OISE and now delivers an interdisciplinary studies programme at The York School in Toronto. In an article published by the Council for Outdoor Educators of Ontario, Sara explored the impact of experiential education on student learning with an emphasis on character development. In co-writing this book, Sara enjoyed the opportunity to continue examining personal growth through another lens. Sara lives in Toronto in a full house with her partner, their two children, a new puppy, her parents, their senior terrier and a niece living abroad from Mexico.

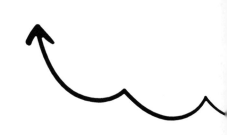

Lightning Source UK Ltd.
Milton Keynes UK
UKHW032209031022
409859UK00006B/1160

9 780995 864627